Guest Pass:

Access To Your Teen's World

Susan Oh Cha, Ph.D.

Yumi Bryana Cha

LifeNote Press

Cover and interior design by Daria Lacy

Author photographs by Mindy Webb

ISBN 978-0-9836551-0-7

Printed in the United States of America

A Note to the Reader

Many of the examples in this book are fictionalized composites based on real stories shared with either or both of the authors. Some are actual experiences of the adolescents who answered the survey, quoted with their permission for this book.

In order to avoid cumbersome references to both genders (i.e., he/she, his/her) when speaking in the singular, the authors alternate between the genders. The authors have tried to maintain a gender balance throughout the book with equal references to males and females.

How this book is organized: Each chapter begins with a question that the authors asked teenagers in a confidential survey. Then, "*Mom Susan*" speaks from her perspective as a parent to the question. This is followed by "**Teen Yumi**" who answers the question from her own as well as other adolescents' experiences. "Dr. Susan" once again shares her viewpoint, but this time, focusing on her expertise as a clinical psychologist. Each chapter closes with self-reflective exercises and an application section for the parents.

By wisdom a house is built,
and through understanding it is established;
Through knowledge its rooms are filled
with rare and beautiful treasures.

Proverbs 24:3-4 (NIV)

Contents

Prelude

A Day in the Life of a Teenager

The alarm goes off, but I don't budge. I push the snooze button and keep sleeping. I'm so tired. I hate waking up at 6:30 a.m. every morning. Ugh! That loud alarm again. I push the snooze button a second time. Soon after, my mom walks in and says, "Good morning sweetie!" How can she be so cheerful?!? I'm not like this. I'm usually kind of grumpy in the mornings, particularly when school is the reason for getting up. I ignore my mom. I wonder why school has to start this early. It makes more sense for it to start later: 11 a.m. sounds good to me and my friends.

Eventually I wake up. I "sleep walk" over to the bathroom, brush my teeth, wash my face, and change. I think about what I have to do today and who I'm going to see. If I'm going to see someone that I want to look good for, I dress to impress. Otherwise, I ask my brother what the weather is, and I throw on random clothes based on his answer. I put on my makeup and curl my bangs. I don't use a lot of makeup, just mascara and a little bit of eye shadow. After fussing over how I look, I go downstairs to eat breakfast.

We leave the house around 6:50 a.m. I have "0 period" P.E. It starts at 7 a.m. My mom drops me off in front of the girl's locker room, so it's convenient for me. As she leaves, sometimes, I wave goodbye (when I'm in a good mood), and sometimes, I just walk off (when I'm irritated). I'm annoyed at my mom on some mornings, because we get into a conversation during the ride over to school where she will not give me permission to do something I want to do. I wish I could do whatever I want!

No matter my mood with my mom, when I see my friends, I become happy. I wave and yell, "Hi!" They greet me the same way. After my friends and I change in the locker room, we link arms, and we skip to class. For some reason, we're all so hyper and excited even though it's so early. As class goes on, we start getting bored and can't wait for the period to be over. "Legit" classes then begin. From class to class, I walk with different people. Some classes I actually look forward to going to, others I don't. I would take the time to explain each class, but I don't think you want to hear all the details.

After school, I meet with my close group of friends. It's usually a group of four or five of us. We hang out in the quad and just talk about how our day was. Sometimes we make spontaneous plans like going on frozen yogurt runs or spending the afternoon at one of our houses. When we're together, we eat, nap, talk, and watch TV. Today, because it's Friday, we decide to go downtown and hang out there. We take the public bus and the light rail. It's interesting to see various people and hear their conversations on the bus. When we arrive, we eat at Johnny Rockets and then go to Quickly for milk tea. Too soon, I have to tell my friends that we have to figure out the public transportation schedule, because I need to get home. I have a curfew that is earlier than others – I hate that! I feel bad making my friends go home when I have to. Also, I like staying out at night with my friends, because it's an escape from my real world of doing homework, practicing music, writing, and studying.

After I come home, I practice my music for about 30 minutes. I don't like practicing, but I love performing with groups. I know I have to practice in order to perform well, but I always argue with my mom about practicing anyway. Theoretically, when I'm finished studying, I can go on Facebook, AIM, and Tumblr. Actually, this usually never happens, because I'm almost always studying late. Around 12 a.m., I have to go to sleep even though I don't want to. I love staying up late and sleeping in. But tomorrow is another day, and I guess I should rest. It's funny how I want to be awake when I should be sleeping and to sleep when I should be awake. I set my alarm. Hopefully, I will be able to hear it in the morning. If not, there's always my mom...

Do pieces of this teenager's day sound familiar? Although each parent, teen, and relationship is unique, there are also common struggles that exist during this developmental stage. We can explore together to come to a clearer understanding of who they are, who we are, and how we can connect more meaningfully. As you read this book, our hope is that you can see yourself in what is being discussed. This can be used as a launching pad for more personal discussions which will further your knowledge and wisdom with which to love your teen.

I have worked for many years as a psychologist with numerous parents who have felt confused, frustrated, and angry with their adolescents. They are not alone: Many of us struggle with our teens on an almost daily basis. What is supposed to be a loving connection more often feels like an adversarial relationship.

I am also a mom of two teenagers – one of whom you have already met. It has been one of my life's greatest joys and challenges to be a mom, especially of teens. When I attend to who my kids are and seek to understand them, they enjoy my company. I am also more likely to find them delightful and wonderful. On the other hand, when I focus primarily on my own agenda and emphasize expediency, they find me controlling, annoying, aggravating, or irrelevant. When our interactions are mostly based on what I need or want from my kids, they frequently leave us both feeling frustrated and disconnected.

While we invest our resources to provide for our teens, how many of us really spend time getting to know them? For many, it is easier to give them what they want (e.g., money, rides, and latest "must-haves") than to invest the necessary time and energy to forge a meaningful relationship, where you know them and you are known by them. Even as we resent being treated like vending machines by our kids, we perpetuate this system, because it is a simpler exchange.

There is less conflict, more positive feelings in the moment, and less thought required.

Parents can sometimes treat their children like vending machines too. We input our "we-know-best" advice, and we expect "you-are-right-dad" output. While this sounds like a welcome change from the usual arguments you might get into with your teens, it makes for unhealthy people and relationships. Of course, it is important to give our resources to our kids. This type of interaction can be one piece – not the whole – of the puzzle that is our relationship. In order to have a meaningful connection with our teens, it is essential to make efforts to know and understand them.

There are also those parents who truly desire to know their teens and want to utilize their time and energy toward this endeavor. However, they are faced with teenagers who refuse to engage, let alone invite them, into their world. There may be various reasons for this: Adolescents can feel invaded by their parents' controlling behaviors, mistrusted by their parents' constant questions, annoyed by their parents' seemingly outdated perspectives, and afraid of their parents' reactions if they shared what was really going on in their lives. Given some of their experiences, it is not surprising that teens not only close the door but lock it.

Here is an opportunity to glimpse what your teens may be thinking, feeling, and doing. Armed with this information, you may be able to unlock the door that has been shut in your face by your adolescents. As a spokesperson for the parents, I will ask about issues that have baffled parents over the years. Yumi and I selected the questions that you see in this book after informally surveying parents to find out what they would like to know.

We then asked teens to answer these questions. As an ambassador of the adolescent group, Yumi will be our "tour guide" as we journey into the teen world. In order to give you a more representative sampling of teenagers, we asked her friends and acquaintances from various places (online social networks, churches, and schools) for their responses. This survey is not meant to provide empirical data. Instead, it is an informal and anecdotal snapshot of the respondents' perspectives.

Each chapter begins with a question that was asked, followed by my contribution from the parent's standpoint. Yumi then answers the question from the teen's point of view, which is analyzed by me – this time, from a psychologist's viewpoint. Each chapter closes with self-reflective exercises and an application section with action items for the parents.

Chapter 1

Privacy and Exposure

*Why are teens so concerned
about privacy with their parents,
and yet broadcast their lives
on social networks?*

As parents, we can feel rejected, hurt, and angry by our kids' need for privacy. We have loved them through their infancy, toddlerhood, and childhood. We want to continue knowing, protecting, and guiding them through adolescence. How can we do this if they shut us out?

As I was watching the San Francisco Giants vs. Texas Rangers World Series, it occurred to me that many of us are used to being in the infield of our children's world. As they get older, we are relegated to the outfield at best and to the ballpark parking lot at worst. Perhaps we are perpetually left in the concession stands with our kids stopping by only when they need or want something.

Many of us are being treated as if we are an irrelevant part of our teens' lives to be endured. On many occasions, I have told my teens to not behave as if I am "an object to be used." I feel like this when they have asked for rides to the mall, and as soon as we get in the car, they promptly put on their earphones for their iPods. It is as if I exist solely as a chauffeur, and they do not need to converse or relate to me in any way. I exist just as an extension of them with no thoughts and feelings of my own.

To add insult to injury, while our teenagers keep their more personal lives secret from us, the parents, they are very open to sharing with their friends online. It is difficult to understand why they would act this way. We have no doubt in our minds that we care more about them than their friends ever can. We have and will always be there for them unlike some of their friends. We know more about our kids and have more life experiences. So, aren't we the best people to hear about their issues and help them?

And yet, our teens do not turn to us. They share all kinds of information in person as well as online with their friends. The latter causes even more angst for us. To reveal personal information on sites that are for public consumption feels scary. There are lots of disturbed people in cyberspace that our children can potentially attract even when safeguards are in place. Thus, we are left often feeling frustrated and worried about our teens. If only we knew what was going on with them...

WE ARE AFRAID

Most of us keep our lives private from our parents, but share our stories with our friends openly. There are many reasons for this. First of all, some of us are afraid of what our parents will think if they find out who we really are. I think parents don't like our desire for privacy because they see this as a way for us to push them out of our lives.

Actually, it's about how many of us believe that we aren't good enough. We're worried that our parents won't like what they see: They may be disappointed in us. So, we hide the truth from them. Sometimes our parents have a certain image of us in their heads that is used to protect them from the reality of who we really are. We keep things private to ensure that this image doesn't change.

In contrast, we're open with our friends, because they're on par with us. This means that they are just as good or bad as us. We keep secrets from our parents not only to protect them but also to avoid judgment and punishment. It's easier to hide what we think, feel, and do from our parents, rather than have to deal with their disappointment, anger, or sadness.

On the other hand, our friends think and act like us. That's why it's easier to express ourselves with them. I know that teenagers can get into lots of "drama," which can be really annoying, but we can handle this. What we find more difficult is dealing with parent "drama," which happens when they are really upset. This usually leads to unreasonable consequences.

Our friends don't have the same authority that parents have: They can't punish us the way parents can. Therefore, it's much more comfortable to share with our friends whatever we think and feel.

WE DON'T WANT TO BE CONTROLLED

Another reason for hiding our lives from our parents but being open with our friends involves our need for freedom. Some teens worry that if they "give an inch," their parents will "take a mile." So, if we give one piece of information, our parents will not be satisfied; instead, they will want the whole story. If we give them the whole truth, they may not like what they hear. And then they will check on us more and become more controlling. This is definitely not what we want.

For example, teenagers cuss a lot: Do our parents want to hear that? No! Would they try to control us and make us stop? Yes! We don't want to be controlled. We want to make our own choices. We like being independent and trying to figure things out on our own. In contrast to our parents, our friends don't tell us what to do. They don't have the power to stop us from doing what we want.

WE ARE LEARNING TOGETHER WITH FRIENDS

Finally, we keep parts of our lives secret from our parents but not our friends, because all of us teens are in the process of figuring out who we are together. Since we're on the same road of finding ourselves, we find it helpful to experience everyday life with friends who are going through the same things.

Our parents may have faced situations like ours, but it was a long time ago – different generation and culture. We don't think they can understand us. So, it's easier not to deal with their opinions about who we should be. Instead, we decide to figure this out by ourselves and with our friends.

EXPOSURE THROUGH SOCIAL MEDIA

Majority of adolescents use social networking sites such as Facebook. Latest statistics indicate that over 73% of teens use these sites to stay connected to their friends.[1] To parents, it seems like they are on these sites 24-7 broadcasting what they are doing – from the tedious to the extraordinary.

One summer, our family went on vacation to the East Coast, visiting multiple states. My husband and I informed only those who needed to know that we would be out of town. At some point during the trip, Yumi volunteered the information that her Facebook status was "New York!" and in fact, her status was changing in tandem with where we were and what we were doing. She was keeping her then 500 "friends" informed of her activities (and ours!).

It would be mind-numbing to hear all the information that teens put out there. However, it would be nice to be in the loop about people who are important to them, interactions that are noteworthy, events that are significant in their lives, and their thoughts and feelings about these. While they do not hesitate to reveal themselves to their peers, they zealously guard their privacy from parents. Why?

CAN PARENTS HANDLE THE TRUTH?

As Yumi describes above, teens are afraid of what their parents will think if they are privy to the inner lives of their teens. The good news: Parents are still important and significant during adolescence, and their opinions matter.[2] The bad news: When adolescents think, feel, and behave in ways that they think are less than ideal, they hide. They may believe, like the Jack Nicholson's character in *A Few Good Men* (1992), that parents "can't handle the truth."

One teen describes how he hides junk food in his room from his mom, who is a health food fanatic. This way, she does not get upset, and he continues to supplement her nutritious food with what he likes to eat. Perhaps it is also the case of the kids not being able to handle the confrontation that will ensue if they try to fight for what they want.

Some teenagers want to guard their parents' images of them. Many parents live in denial about who their kids are and what they may be doing. We all like to believe that it is that other child who is the bad influence, not ours. Because of their parents' lack of desire to really see them for who they are, adolescents collude with their parents to keep their images intact. This then obviously necessitates hiding information from the parents.

FEAR OF JUDGMENT

There are other teens who keep their lives private from their parents for fear of judgment and punishment. I have heard numerous accounts of parents who react badly to revelations by their kids.

For example, a teen shared with her dad that her friend at school was pregnant. The dad's response went something like this – "What?!? She's only 16! I didn't know she was such a bad kid. How can she do this to her parents? She has ruined not only her life but her parents' lives. How can they face their family and friends? Are you having sex too? If you get pregnant, don't think about coming home!" This dad reacted with intense judgment and threats.

Although we can understand the fear that perhaps drove him to make these remarks, all that his daughter hears is condemnation. This leads to her becoming more resolved to not share her struggles with her dad.

In addition, adolescents, like many adults, want to avoid facing consequences of their bad choices for as long as possible. If the household rules are clear, then teens know when they have broken them. They hide their behaviors with the hope that they will not be found out, and thus, not be disciplined. Given these factors, it is understandable that they do not reveal themselves to their parents, only to their friends.

WHAT DO SOCIAL NETWORKING SITES PROVIDE?

Teens feel a sense of freedom and equality with their peers that they do not with their parents. The social networking sites increase this experience of being empowered agents of their own world. Adolescents can create and control the settings in these sites to make it a world that they want to inhabit. They can decide who, what, when, where, and how to share.

They can also choose to "dump and run." They can blog what they want and then leave the site until they decide to read and reply to the responses. They can chat about the day's events, relationships, rumors, plans for social events, and secrets.

Many people report feeling more open and uninhibited on-line than in person.[3] The combination of self-focus and unseen audience cause kids to be less self-conscious, less accountable, and more self-revealing. Teenagers are more likely to use profanity, make aggressive remarks, and/or explore their sexuality (e.g., post inappropriate pictures of themselves and/or others) in ways they would not in person. They may frequently overstate their case, which would horrify parents were they to hear them, but their peers take it in stride.

Adolescents use these sites and friends to explore who they are, what they like, what they want, and who they will be. Social media helps teens process through their thoughts and feelings in their own space. The internet is especially attractive to youths who are shy, socially anxious, and have trouble connecting with their peers face to face: It provides a less vulnerable forum to find others who share their perceptions and experiences.

Teenagers are exploring their identities and coming to terms with who they are and how they feel about themselves through the online sites. They share this journey with their friends since the latter are going through the same development. Together, they are figuring out the "me" and the "not me."

DEVELOPMENTAL CHANGES IN ADOLESCENCE

Teens are encountering significant neurological and physiological changes which impact their emotional and relational experiences. During the adolescent years, the frontal lobe – an area of the brain involved in organization, planning, and judgment – is not fully developed. Because of this, teenagers do not have the same decision-making abilities adults (in general) exhibit.[4] Thus, they are more likely to act impulsively, not consider the consequences of their actions, and engage in more risky behaviors.

In addition, teens are experiencing tremendous physiological growth. There are hormonal and physical changes that impact their experiences of themselves and others. There is a sense of solidarity and a belonging among teenagers, because they are on the same journey to adulthood. Parents are not. Thus, teens do not trust that parents can relate to where they are and who they are. So, it is reasonable for them not to share as much with parents as with their friends.

REFLECTIONS

A. In what ways can you recognize yourself and/or your teens in this chapter?

Me: _____

My teens: _____

B. On a scale of 1 to 10 (with 1 = not at all and 10 = completely), how open are your teenagers with information? _____

What could you live with? _____

What do you think your teens could live with? _____

C. If your teens tend to keep information from you, why do you think that is? Check what fits your experience or fill in the blank.

☐ Fear of Judgment

☐ Avoidance of Punishment

☐ Protection of Their Images

☐ Desire for Freedom

☐ Need for Control

☐ Development of Their Identities

Other _____

D. Can you reflect on why your kids may think and feel this way?

_____

_____

E. How are your teenagers using social networks like Facebook and Tumblr?

_____

_____

F. How much information do your teens post on these sites?

_____

_____

G. How do you feel about this?

_____

_____

FROM KNOWLEDGE TO ACTION

A. Remember that your thoughts and feelings matter even if it seems as if your teens do not care, listen, nor want you in their lives. It is important to continue to be open and willing to dialogue with your kids in spite of their apparent negative attitudes.

B. Do not personalize their request for privacy from you. This just leads to a vicious cycle of anger and defensiveness between you and your teens. Their need for privacy is not about rejecting or hurting you as much as it is about their need for separation to explore their identities.

C. Talk to your teenagers about the issues that may have come up for you as you read this chapter:

1. If you think that the question addressed in this chapter is valid for your teens, ask, "Why are you so concerned about privacy with me, and yet broadcast your life on social networks?" Compare their answers with other teenagers' responses shared by Yumi.

2. If your kids seem open to discussing this further, ask, "Do you think I respect your need for privacy?" If they answer monosyllabically, follow up with "How do I show respect? How do I not?"

3. You can share your feelings about this privacy/exposure issue, and then ask, "Can you understand where I am coming from?"

4. If your teenagers are spending too much time on the social media sites, and they are emotionally immature and socially awkward, then be aware that they may be more likely to share inappropriate information and/or be negatively influenced by peers online. While the internet provides a "safer" place to explore who they are and what they want to be, it can also be more "dangerous" given their vulnerabilities.

5. It is important to discuss how you and your teen can respect each other's needs. Come to mutually agreeable decisions regarding how you will respect his privacy and how he will respect your desire to protect and guide him safely through adolescence. For

example, perhaps you agree to allow him to use Facebook as long as you can be his "friend." You can further negotiate other terms of social media use (e.g., when, where, and how long).

Chapter 2

"Chatting" about "Nothing" for Hours

What do teens "chat" about,
especially when parents are not around?

Have you ever noticed that your teens have plenty to say to their friends? Their favorite words to you may be "I don't know," "Fine," and "Nothing," but to their friends, they seem to have more quantity and quality of words at their disposal.

Recently, I saw a commercial in which a mom is talking to her teenage son who is texting on his phone. She asks him, "Who are you talking to?" He answers, "No one." She then inquires, "What are you talking about?" He responds, "Nothing." She follows with, "When you are done talking about nothing with no one, come down to dinner."

When I overhear my teens' conversations at times, I am struck by the ordinariness of the exchanges. However, when I cannot hear what they are sharing, I cannot help but wonder: Who are they talking to? What are they disclosing? Are they revealing personal matters that I would rather they do not? Can I trust them to be wise about what they share and with whom?

Sometimes kids immediately stop what they are doing when parents enter their space where they are texting, instant messaging, and/or posting with their friends. Apparently, even when they are not talking about anything particularly important or incriminating, there is an automatic reflex of concealing their activities. When this happens with my kids, I become even more curious to know what they are discussing. So, what are they saying to each other?

THIS AND THAT

It depends on the teen as well as whom they are in conversation with. For example, some kids are quiet and shy, and so they tend to keep their thoughts and feelings inside, instead of expressing them. Some teenagers who are Christians talk about their faith, relationships with God, and church issues, mostly with other Christian teens. Others who are into games, such as Call of Duty and Star Craft, discuss stats (e.g., who has the most kills). Teens who watch and/or play sports debate about the best players and teams. When the San Francisco Giants won the 2010 World Series, some kids could not stop talking about it. Those of us who love to shop share information about the latest fashions and newest cool stores.

EVERYDAY CONVERSATIONS

While we have differences in what we chat about at times, we also have similarities in our everyday conversations. We discuss topics that range from being boring and superficial to being interesting and important.

We talk about media, school issues, crushes, family problems, and emotional concerns. We chat about what we like and dislike about certain tv episodes and movies. We also love to share our opinions about music and artists. When we find entertaining clips on YouTube, we send these to our friends.

We also share our feelings about school – our teachers, our grades, the amount of homework, and the clubs. It makes us feel better to vent about these issues with our friends who are going through these same experiences.

One of the main topics that we chat about when our parents aren't around involves infatuations. Girls gossip about boys – who's cute and who's not. Boys rate girls based on their looks – who's hot and who's not. We can talk for hours about who likes who, who broke up with who, who's doing what with who, etc.

DIFFICULT DISCUSSIONS

Not only do we discuss trivial stuff, we also talk about critical issues. Some teens have family problems, such as dealing with parents who fight all the time, who are separating, and who are divorced. Teenagers share how their parents do alcohol and drugs which make them feel unsafe and anxious. Kids who have parents who are really strict, mean, and even maybe abusive talk about how frustrated and angry they are at their parents.

Other emotional concerns that we talk about include peer pressure to drink and do drugs, image issues, sleep problems, depression, and anxiety. We'll discuss this more in the next chapter where we focus on problems that teenagers have.

TEENS ARE NOT SO DIFFERENT FROM ADULTS

Given that our kids seem to go mute when we are around, we would expect that they are communicating about something salacious and perhaps even forbidden. But as Yumi shows us, teenagers are not so different from adults.

Like us, their personalities, backgrounds, and interests determine what and how something is communicated. Who or what group they are with also governs what they share. However, there are differences in how information is communicated by teens vs. parents. These include subject variances, levels of transparency in these topics, and choices of communication systems.

SIMILARITIES IN CONVERSATIONS

Similar to adults, what teens chat about is decided by various factors. Our personalities serve as boundaries within which we converse. For example, if an individual is extroverted (i.e., someone who is energized by being with people, seeks stimulation, needs to process her thoughts verbally, and likes immediate sharing and feedback), she is more likely to chat about everything to lots of people.

On the other hand, if a teen is introverted (i.e., someone who is drained when he is around people for too long, seeks quiet, likes his own space, and needs to process information internally prior to sharing), he is more likely to keep his thoughts and feelings to himself. When he does share, he may do so with a chosen few.

Another personality trait that impacts what and how one communicates involves one's disposition. If a teen is optimistic, i.e., views the world in hopeful and positive ways, she is more likely to express and respond confidently. In contrast, if an individual is pessimistic, i.e., views the world in "glass half-empty" and distrustful ways, he is more likely to communicate with negativity.

Not only our personalities but our personal circumstances and experiences influence what we talk about with others. Yumi describes how one's faith shapes one's conversation. If a teen is a Christian, she may be concerned with what it means to be a Christian and how to deepen her relationship with God.

Many adolescents who are of Asian heritage may commiserate together on the old-world mentality and values of their immigrant parents. Others who are suffering physically or emotionally may discuss these issues in order to understand what is happening, get support, and find a solution.

Obviously, our interests will also influence what we talk about – whether one is a teen or an adult. As Yumi mentions, kids who are interested in shopping enjoy gossiping about when and where to shop. They compare styles and prices. They share their excitement over great bargains: They are not so different from adults.

Others who are passionate about books converse about what they have read, why they like/dislike certain books/authors, and any noteworthy passages in books. Some are absorbed in the latest video games, which then dominates the chatting via texts, online, and in person.

Additionally, who we are talking to makes a difference to what we choose to share. Like adults, if teens are talking to their best friends, they may open up about personal issues, from family problems to sex. If they are with a group of acquaintances, they may discuss the latest movies and music that they like. If they are with people that they want to impress (with their knowledge, popularity, maturity, etc.), they may share their "accomplishments" (good and bad), even exaggerate them, in order to get the kind of accolades they want.

DIFFERENCES IN COMMUNICATION

Although what adolescents chat about is familiar to adults because we talk about similar things, there are also differences. Teenagers are more likely to chat about certain topics due to their developmental stage in life. Thus, subjects for discussions may center on issues related to identity exploration, school, peer pressures, romantic interests, drugs/alcohol, and sex.

Among these, romantic interests appear to dominate many of the teens' thoughts, feelings, and conversations. There is always news to report on this front due to the general tendency of adolescents to have short-lived infatuations and relationships.

Furthermore, teenagers are much more transparent about what they share than adults. This is consistent with their impulsivity, self-absorption, and decreased understanding of potential consequences of certain revelations. They are also more trusting of each other. These characteristics lead to many teens sharing personal details that most parents would not.

As we grow older, we may become more guarded and careful about what, how, and with whom we share. To a certain extent, we lose our childlike faith due to increased knowledge of people and experience of painful life events. Of course, we also have learned to curtail our impulses.

become less egocentric, and have better understanding of how current choices can impact our future. These factors contribute to decreased transparency in adults.

Another difference is the communication tools used. Parents are more likely to meet face to face (especially regarding more personal matters) and/or pick up the phone to dialogue. We usually have a specific reason for calling or wanting to meet. There is a beginning, middle, and end to our conversations.

Teenagers, on the other hand, need a medium that is more conducive to constant checking in and out of friends' lives in the midst of going to school, doing homework, and participating in extra-curricular activities. Thus, they are more likely to pick up the phone to text, use a mouse to AIM and post on Facebook, and turn to other social media to chat with their friends.

These ways of communicating lend itself to continuous stream of background chatter as they go about their days. It is indeed true sometimes that our teenagers are talking to "no one" (person) about "nothing" (special).

REFLECTIONS

A. What do you think your teenagers talk about when you are not there?

_____

_____

B. How are your conversations similar to and different from your teens' chats?

Similar: _____

_____

Different: _____

_____

C. Do you have a clear boundary regarding what information you would or would not exchange? Yes ☐ No☐

and <u>with whom </u>you would or would not disclose? Yes☐ No ☐

List a few people and the topics (e.g., work, relationships, and finances) you feel comfortable sharing with each one:

_____

_____

_____

List any issues you usually do not talk to anyone about:

_____

_____

D. Can you answer the above question for your teenagers?

_____

_____

E. What are your reactions to your teens' continuous stream of background chatter with their friends?

_____

_____

FROM KNOWLEDGE TO ACTION

A. Although your teenagers seem to be so different from you, keep in mind that your teens are like you in many respects. Just as you are not one-dimensional, neither are they. They are complex: similar to other adolescents yet different, have outside responsibilities and commitments that impact their lives at home, and talk about issues that run the whole gamut (from the trivial to the significant).

B. When you enter their room and see them clicking to a different screen on their computer, do not jump to the conclusion that they are looking at inappropriate sites, "chatting" with their friends, and/or divulging secrets. This assumption can lead to defensiveness and unnecessary conflicts.

C. Engage your teenagers in conversation:

1. Ask the question that we posed, "What do you chat about, especially when I am not around?"

2. Most likely, you might get a one-word answer, such as, "Nothing." This can make you feel frustrated, which is understandable, but persevere and follow up with, "How do you think you are different in what you share when I am in the room vs. when I am not?"

3. Let your kids know that it is appropriate for them to have their own conversations and that you do not expect them to report back to you. However, you are interested in their lives, and whenever they would like to share, you would welcome the opportunity to listen.

4. Communicate with your teens the importance of choosing wisely (a) <u>what</u> they decide to disclose and (b) <u>with whom</u> they choose to share – especially their more personal thoughts and feelings. You might discuss with them names of kids and adults you both know and trust that they can freely talk to. Make sure to choose family members and friends who are nonjudgmental listeners who can keep confidences well.

5. You might consider sharing whom you trust to be <u>your</u> confidante

and why. In addition, you can give examples of what issues you would feel comfortable revealing and what you would not.

Chapter 3

Teen Troubles

*What kinds of problems
do teens usually experience?*

*P*arents hear lots of alarming stories of youths having problems, especially in the media. Just in the past year, there have been numerous reported cases of teen sexual assaults, suicides, and deaths related to driving under the influence of alcohol/drugs in our "nice" and "safe" neighborhoods.

When I hear about these heartbreaking stories, I want to (a) pretend that they have nothing to do with me and distance myself from them or (b) overwhelm myself with "what if's" and hover over my kids even more than I do. Neither of these is a healthy response. When we have more knowledge of what the teenage world is like, we are better prepared to handle these types of information.

In addition to tragedies like those above, there are also troubles that teens experience on a daily basis. These are the issues that may not seem to be significant at the outset but could potentially lead to the devastating news like the ones above. Since so many adolescents are reluctant to share their problems with their parents, Yumi and I thought it would be helpful to ask the above question of teens and listen to what they have to share.

TYPICAL DIFFICULTIES

*T*here are many different kinds of challenges that teens experience. Typical problems that teens face include academic anxieties, over-packed schedules, relationship issues, self-image concerns, and peer pressures. Not that surprising really.

ACADEMIC STRESS

Many teenagers, especially Juniors and Seniors, are stressed about their grades, college applications, and SAT/ACT scores. This is because everyone says that our future depends upon what we do in high school. No wonder we are stressed! Some of us are in really competitive schools which makes it difficult to get the straight A's that we want.

The pressure to do well works against us too. Sometimes we can't do well on tests because of this pressure. When one student is nervous, it leads to others being even more stressed out. It's tough to get good grades under these circumstances. Many students take accelerated classes in order to look better on the college applications. When one friend enrolls in these types of classes, the other feels pressure to do more academically to keep up.

OVER-SCHEDULED

In addition, we're involved with competitive sports and other extra-curricular activities. Between academics and all the other stuff that we have to do, our schedules are packed. These commitments may be more than we can handle: We often stay up as late as 2am finishing homework and studying. This then causes us to be exhausted in the morning, and so, some of us drink caffeinated beverages to stay awake and alert in school.

RELATIONSHIP ISSUES

One of the biggest problems among teenagers revolves around relationships. When you hear the word, "relationship," what comes to mind? When I hear this word, I tend only to think of romantic relationships. I don't usually think about parent-child or friend-friend relationships. However, all of these relationships can make us stressed.

PARENT-TEEN STRUGGLES

First, let's talk about our relationships with our parents. Many teens don't have good relationships with their parents. We fight about almost everything: curfew, choice of friends, school performance, dating, not spending enough time with family, caring only about friends, being online too much, the way we dress, etc.

Sometimes parents can be really mean. For example, I have heard stories of parents telling their children that they are ugly and fat. How do parents expect their kids to be respectful and obedient to them when they say things like that?!? Parents have also said these awful words to their kids:

"You the most ungrateful, selfish child ever born!"
"Why aren't you like so and so?"
"What are you doing with your life?"
"What's the matter with you? Are you that stupid?"

These comments hurt and anger their kids which cause them to grow further apart from their parents. Teens then turn to their friends. Some examples of what teens have expressed include:

"I'm sick of having to be perfect!"
"I don't care about anyone in this house!"
"I want to run away! It's not like they care anyways."
"I wish I had different parents."
"My parents are so stupid!"
"My parents don't let me do anything I want to do!"
"All they care about is what they care about."

Sometimes teens will remark on how much they hate their parents and how they wish their parents would die.

Parents, don't be shocked by these words. Many think and feel these things just at the moment. These statements are ways that kids express their frustrations with their parents when they don't get their way, when they are being nagged, and when they feel misunderstood.

Many of us feel a lot of pressure to be perfect. When our parents get mad at us for whatever reason, we feel sad and resentful. We would like encouragement, not just one lecture after another on achieving and maintaining high standards for ourselves and for them.

FRIENDSHIP TROUBLES

Not only do teenagers have problems with their parents, they also face painful situations with their friends. Maintaining strong connections with friends is really important to us, and so when we have difficulties with friends, we get worried.

Sometimes, we get close to one friend, and then this friend drifts away. This can make us feel rejected and expendable. We are left wondering why this happened. In addition, other kids make comments, such as, "How come you aren't hanging out with so and so anymore?" We don't like hearing these remarks, because they bring attention to us and bring back hurtful memories.

Other times, kids get mad at their friends for gossiping behind their backs and spreading rumors. For example, one teen says to another, "Did you hear that this girl and this boy made out?" When someone is the subject of gossip in school, it's tough for that person to act normal. It's really hurtful and embarrasing.

There are kids who become friends for a certain reason, e.g., to use one friend to meet another friend. When this is found out, it can also lead to bad feelings. Obviously, this will cause the friendship to end.

From time to time, friends have problems with each other, but they pretend that everything is perfect. Since many of us hate confronting, it's easier to try to forget about the problems. When we do this, we end up with a pile of unresolved issues. This can lead to a huge fight which can fix or end the friendship later on.

Competition between friends also can cause difficulties. At times, our friends can make us feel stupid. If they know more, are taking harder classes, and/or use bigger vocabulary, we may think that we're not smart enough for them. Other ways friends compete with one another involves looks, popularity, athletic abilities, etc. If one friend is better than another at something, then that friendship can break. I guess we don't really know how to handle some of the feelings that we have.

LOVE PROBLEMS

One of the biggest problems that teenagers face has to do with romantic relationships. There are issues of trust, jealousy, cheating, lying, miscommunication, and one-way love.

For example, there is a girl who likes this guy in school. He was known to be a flirt, but she didn't care in the beginning. They started going out. After awhile, she became jealous about his conversations with other girls, especially online. She read a post on his Facebook wall that implied that he had cheated on her. Instead of confronting him, she kept her feelings of betrayal and upset bottled up inside. She realized that she liked him more than he liked her. In fact, she couldn't tell that he liked her at all. Even though it was hard, she decided to break up with him.

When kids fight and/or end their relationships, they are tearful, distracted from school, and depressed. Some even think about suicide. Depending on how much kids were into their relationships, these thoughts and feelings may last from days to months.

Parents can also make relationship issues worse. If they disapprove of their teens having a boyfriend/girlfriend, these kids will hide their relationships. They end up lying, going behind their parents' backs, and then feeling guilty. If parents don't like their teens' choice of a boyfriend/girlfriend, then there may be lots of tension in the family.

SELF-IMAGE CONCERNS

Self-image issues are common among many teens. How we feel about our looks influences how we think and feel about ourselves. Many girls think that they aren't skinny enough. They compare themselves with celebrities like Jessica Alba and Megan Fox. They can starve themselves or throw up, even from middle school, to look thinner and better. But no matter what they do, they continue to feel bad about themselves.

Many guys who are overweight, too short, or too skinny, also struggle with their self-image. They don't feel self-confident, because girls don't want to go out with them. People have their own opinion on what's hot and what's not. I think that everyone has his unique look: We all can look good in our own way.

Not only are appearances important to one's self-image, but also our talents. For example, how gifted we are in sports and/or music impact our self-worth. Some of us are better than others in various areas. Those of us who are not as gifted may feel bad. Self-esteem is also affected by how smart we are. When a student isn't taking advanced classes in a school where this is expected, this teen may feel stupid. The situation is worse when parents also expect their children to get perfect grades and scores, but they don't.

Whether we have friends or not also influence how we feel about ourselves. If a teen is home alone on a Friday night not by choice but because she isn't invited to hang out, then she would feel like a loner. When we're having fun with our friends, we feel wanted, and that feels good. Everything that happens to us pretty much affects how we feel about ourselves.

PEER PRESSURE

Teenagers often face peer pressure involving alcohol, drugs, and sex. Many kids attend parties where alcohol is present. This leads to a dilemma for some teens: To drink or not to drink? If someone chooses not to have alcohol, he is seen as a loser. He will be teased and pressured to drink. If someone wants to fit in and be accepted, she may decide to drink even if she thinks it's wrong. Peer pressure to drink doesn't occur only at parties. When kids are stressed, they are more likely to say "yes" to their "friends" in any situation.

This is also true for drugs. When teens are depressed, upset, bored, or lonely, they are more open to the idea of drugs as a way to feel better. If they are around other kids who do drugs, they feel more pressured to do the same. Sometimes, kids come to school on drugs, and they get attention from their peers. Teachers do not seem to notice, but students gossip about who is coming to school stoned.

Sex is another area where peer pressure can affect teens' choices. If a couple has been going out for a while, then one of them may pressure the other to take the next step. In order to keep the relationship, she may go along with it. Also, couples can feel harassed by other friends to have sex. Guys tend to taunt each other to be more sexual with their girlfriends. Even though someone might not be ready to have sex, he would make the move so that he appears "cool" among his friends. Peer pressure is one of the hardest things for kids to deal with.

STATISTICS ON ADOLESCENT MENTAL DISORDERS

In the above paragraphs, Yumi illustrates typical issues that trouble teenagers. She discusses how teens are stressed due to academic difficulties, over-packed schedules, relationship challenges, self-image issues, and peer pressures. Some are able to manage these pressures well while others cannot. Those who do not cope well with the angst of adolescence may develop mental health difficulties or may exacerbate what is already present (through genetic predispositions and environmental factors, to be discussed more in detail later).

A recent national survey of 10,123 adolescents[5] reveals that about 50% meet the diagnostic criteria for mental health disorders[6] and about 22% experience severe impairment in daily functioning due to their disorders. The researchers found that teenagers whose parents are married or cohabiting show less anxiety and behavior disorders in comparison to those whose parents are separated or divorced.

They also report that the most consistent correlation between mental health problems and parental characteristics involves the latter's education level: Adolescents whose parents are not college educated are at more risk for all types of mental health issues. Keep in mind that there are other numerous factors that contribute to the manifestation of symptoms. The top three conditions reported in this research data are "anxiety," "behavior," and "mood" disorders.

ANXIETY

Everyone experiences anxiety at times. In fact, some amount of anxiety is beneficial to one's functioning: It motivates one to perform tasks and be productive. The normal emotion of anxiety becomes problematic when it becomes constant and interferes with daily functioning. Types of anxiety disorders include panic disorder, posttraumatic stress disorder, social phobia, obsessive compulsive disorder, and specific phobias.

Each of these has specific criteria that need to be met for an individual to be diagnosed. In general, symptoms of anxiety disorders include the following: feelings of fear, uncontrollable thoughts, shortness of breath, agitation, cold or clammy hands/feet, and/or muscle tension. More females than males are diagnosed with anxiety disorders.

Many teens feel anxious when taking a test, performing in public, and confronting someone. Most, if not all, experience feelings of worry and nervousness when dealing with these types of situations. However, not everyone experiences the full range of symptoms required for an anxiety disorder diagnosis nor are their fears considered irrational and overwhelming to the point where they structure their lives to avoid exposure to these feared circumstances.

For example, Yumi discusses how teenagers are stressed by academic pressures. Their stress increases around exams. Many are quite anxious before taking tests, particularly finals.

Their anxiety may be manifested in the following ways: (a) avoiding studying until the last minute, (b) being ritualistic about personal study guidelines, (c) experiencing physiological symptoms, such as rapid heartbeat, as the exam commences, and (d) being unable to recall information studied, especially during the initial phase of the exam where one's nervousness is at its peak.

While these experiences are relatively normal and may not fully meet the criteria for an anxiety disorder, it can still be distressing. It is important to learn how to manage these types of anxiety symptoms in order to prevent further difficulties.

BEHAVIORAL PROBLEMS

Like anxiety, many adolescents also experience normal amounts of behavioral issues. They may occasionally lie, cheat, act impulsively, be truant, or be insolent. However, when these behaviors become a constant source of trouble (especially between teens and authority figures) and are disruptive to daily functioning, then professional assessment and treatment may be required.

Types of behavior disorders include attention-deficit hyperactivity disorder, conduct disorder, and oppositional defiant disorder. These are typically diagnosed for children and adolescents. More boys than girls are usually diagnosed with behavior disorders.

Yumi mentions that one of the major problems that teens experience involves their parents. Countless parent-teen relationships are fraught with anger, resentment, and hostility. Many parents are familiar with their teenagers' outbursts of irritability, disobedience, and rebelliousness. These behaviors need to be understood in the context of each relationship. After all, if teens perceive their parents to be unreasonable, inflexible, or even abusive, it is logical and natural for them to respond in the ways described above.

While teenagers can occasionally express these behaviors, in order to meet the criteria for a clinical diagnosis, such as oppositional defiant disorder, they need to exhibit an ongoing, consistent pattern of extremely negative behaviors towards people in authority. Symptoms include being excessively argumentative, actively noncompliant with rules and adults, and deliberately hateful when upset.

DEPRESSION

Similar to anxiety and behavioral issues, people feel depressed from time to time. It is normal to feel sad or have diminished interest in pleasurable activities when certain life events occur, e.g., end of a relationship. However, when these emotions last more than two weeks, are accompanied by other consistent symptoms, and disrupt one's daily functioning, then it may be a sign of a serious mental disorder.

Unlike adults, teenagers are more likely to express depression through mood fluctuations, irritability, and physical complaints. There are many types of mood disorders, including major depressive disorder, dysthymia, and bipolar disorder. More teen girls than teen boys are diagnosed with mood disorders.

Yumi states that teens suffer from academic, relational, and self-image issues. All of these can contribute to feeling depressed – within or outside the normal range. When a teen has invested so much of her energy and time in a romantic relationship, in making the school's sports team, in getting A's, and/or in having good friends, and if she is not successful in one or more of these endeavors, we could imagine that she would experience some level of depression for a limited time.

She might be moody, unmotivated, tired, and experiencing low self-worth. If these feelings continue for an extended period of time and interfere with her ability to participate in regular activities, then it is important to seek professional assessment and treatment.

NORMAL TO ABNORMAL CONTINUUM

Although most of the adolescents do not experience significant distress to the level that requires intervention in order to function well, it is still important to attend to the issues they do have. Mental disorders can be understood within a continuum from normal to abnormal thoughts, feelings, and behaviors. We all have had experiences of depression and anxiety, i.e., certain features of these disorders although not the disorders themselves.

Genetic predisposition (e.g., parent has one or more mental disorders) and environmental factors (e.g., poverty, loss, traumas) can tip the scale from the normal to the abnormal range. Thus, as we become aware of our children's stressors, we are more in a position to understand and help them cope adaptively, so that they do not develop significant mental health issues.

REFLECTIONS

A. Are your teenagers affected by any of the following?

☐ Academic Anxieties

☐ Over-Packed Schedules

☐ Relational Issues

☐ Self-image Concerns

☐ Peer Pressures

☐ Other _____

In what ways? _____

_____

_____

B. Are your teens exhibiting any of the following signs of distress? Please check all that apply.

☐ Increased Isolation

☐ Apathy or Lack of Interest in Many or Most Activities

☐ Cutting Class

☐ Frequent Illnesses

☐ Loss of Sleep or Oversleeping

☐ Loss of Appetite or Overeating

☐ Sense of Hopelessness and Despair

☐ Anxiety

☐ Drug/Alcohol Use

☐ Impulsive Anger/Rage

☐ Sexual Acting Out

C. Is there a family history of mental illnesses? Yes ☐ No ☐

D. If yes, please list: _____

_____

E. Have there been any significant stressors in your teens' history?
   Yes ☐ No ☐

F. If yes, please list (e.g., developmental concerns, medical issues,
   divorce, abuse, losses, and ongoing conflicts):

_____

_____

FROM KNOWLEDGE TO ACTION

A. All adolescents experience various difficulties. Some are newsworthy while others are not, but all are noteworthy. It is important as parents to be aware of what our teens are struggling with so that we can prevent further suffering.

B. If you answered "yes" to any of the earlier questions and/or checked some of the signs of distress for your teens, it is essential to continue to monitor how they are functioning. These indicate genetic predispositions and environmental factors that increase your teens' risk for developing mental health issues. While it is hard to understand and accept that they may be in trouble beyond what is considered "normal," nonetheless, it is critical to have your teens evaluated and/or treated if you are concerned.

C. In addition to finding professional assistance, you can also do your part to possibly alleviate some of the distress.

　1. Encourage your teenagers to share their experiences with people they trust. Numerous studies have shown the physical and mental health benefits of disclosing our thoughts and feelings to others.[7] By revealing those areas of our lives that feel out of control, ugly, overwhelming, traumatic, and/or even just simply annoying, to someone who listens well, we can manage what is happening to us more effectively. When we inhibit and repress those issues that negatively affect us, we are more likely to get stuck there – ruminate and obsess over what has happened – leading to increased symptoms of poor health.

　　(a) While there are times when Yumi openly shares her hurts with me, more often than not, she's more comfortable sharing with her friends (especially at the outset). I have encouraged her to do so while keeping in mind what we talked about in the earlier chapter regarding how to choose confidantes.

　　(b) If you can, cultivate close and supportive relationships with adults who are invested in your family whom you both like and trust, so that when your teens are in distress, they can go to those individuals when they cannot come to you.

2. Ask your teenagers to journal. Writing can feel safer than talking to someone since there is no chance of judgment and condemnation of your thoughts, feelings, and behaviors. It can lead to deeper expressions of ourselves.

(a) I have often encouraged my patients/clients to do "stream of consciousness" journaling where they write whatever comes to mind about a specific event/thought/feeling that is causing the hurt. If they feel uncomfortable doing this due to the possibility of someone else reading their journals, I ask them to shred it afterward. They can also find resources on the internet for a password protected space for writing.

(b) The act of writing honestly about our concerns helps us to face what is happening, have a better understanding of how we think and feel, and cope with what has and will occur. Most people are driven to make sense of experiences to facilitate healing. Journaling helps us to do that.

3. Assist your children to learn a couple of self-help tools that have been found to be effective in reducing distress: (a) Restructuring Thoughts and (b) Deep Breathing. There are many techniques that are helpful. I have chosen what I consider to be the two of the most effective and easiest to learn.

(a) Restructuring Thoughts:

• Get a personal notebook.

• Write with your teens any negative thoughts they have. For example, "No one cares about me."

• Identify and write down how this thought is illogical and false using specific experiences. Using the above example, you might say, "The other day, your friend gave you a ride to the mall," or "Your friend just texted to get together on the weekend." These are examples that contradict your teens' damaging thought(s) that cause them to feel depressed.

• Impress upon them that their thoughts and feelings are just that – their perceptions – which can be changed to more positive and realistic perspectives.

• Finish by writing down a different thought that is based on reality. For example, "Right now, I don't feel cared for by my friends, Mary and Jane, because they are hanging out without me."

• If the thoughts are valid and real, obviously, you cannot refute them. Being inauthentic is not going to help alleviate pain. Thus, if this is the case, then help your teens face their legitimate thoughts and cope with them. One of the ways in which you can help is to reframe their experiences in order to generate hope and positive change.

> • Pick a framed picture in your room. What is the feeling that picture generates? Now, think of a different frame for that same picture. For example, if you have a traditional, elegant wooden frame, then think of a modern, stark metal frame around it. The picture is the same, but different feelings are evoked when we change the frame.

> • Likewise, your teenagers' thoughts may be based on actual, real interactions with others in which case you cannot refute the thoughts through restructuring. However, you can help them find growth and meaning in the painful experiences by reframing them.

> • For example, you might say to your teenager, "It is really hurtful that your friends invited all but you to the party. And that this has happened not once but on multiple occasions in the past few months. It looks like they are letting you know that they don't want you to be a part of their group. What do you think? Why do you think this happened? What is your responsibility in this? What is theirs? Although it feels bad, can you see how this might be a good thing in the long run?"

(b) Deep Breathing

- Sit with your teenager in a comfortable position.

- Have your teen breathe slowly in through his nose with his mouth closed for a count of three-five seconds. Make sure that his stomach is expanding. Ask him to hold his breath for three-five beats. Then breathe out slowly and strongly (as if he is blowing out a candle) through his mouth for about five-seven seconds. His stomach should contract when he breathes out. Repeat: Do a set of six to twelve deep breaths.

- When your child is doing this exercise, she is consciously relaxing her mind and body, reducing stress, increasing energy, and releasing endorphins (body's natural opiates to decrease pain and increase pleasure).

- It is important to have your teens practice this consistently so that when a perceived crisis occurs, they can use it automatically and naturally to lower their distress.

Chapter 4

Dealing with Friends Who are Suffering

How do teens usually cope with friends who are distressed?

*A*s parents, we have a huge desire to protect our children from any and all potential harm. We want our children's lives to be as free of suffering as we can make it. If their friends are troubled, we are afraid of how this might impact our kids.

Depending on the kind of distress their friends are experiencing, our teenagers may feel angst too. After all, peers influence one another. We wonder about the advisability of allowing these friendships to flourish. While we can sympathize with their friends' difficulties, we do not want our kids to be negatively affected.

Given some of the troubles that teenagers can get into, our kids might not be able to handle them on their own. If our kids tell us what is happening with some of their friends, and they do not want anyone else to know, then this can cause a dilemma for us. We may struggle between our responsibility to our kids who have asked us to keep the information confidential and to fellow parents who need to know the information so that they can help their kids.

For example, if I find out that a teenager is using drugs, and I know that his parents have no idea about this, do I say anything to them? If I was that parent, I would definitely want to know. At the same time, I do not want to lose my children's trust. What do I do? Perhaps what we might choose to do in this situation is determined by what we know of our teens' capacity to deal adaptively with their friends who are in distress.

HANDLING THINGS ON OUR OWN

We don't know what to do when our friends are in trouble. We want to help them, but we can only do so much. One situation involves friends who are distressed but don't open up. If they're really upset but refuse to talk about what is troubling them, then it's even more difficult to help them. Often, we talk among ourselves to think of ways to make our friends (who are hurting) to feel better.

We try for awhile, but eventually, we give up. If this

happens, we may avoid being around those friends, because it feels tense and awkward to be with them. This makes us feel bad. We are sad that they aren't doing well, but there isn't much we can do. We leave them alone until they are ready to open up or they get over whatever is bothering them.

Another scenario is when our friends who are upset are able to talk about what happened. Then, there's more of a chance that we can help them. We can listen. And as Jun (17-year-old senior) says, "boys nod a lot" and "girls often side with their friends" with "lots of, oh yeah, totally."

A lot of times, kids appreciate just having someone by their side. Teens who are troubled feel better when their friends notice that they aren't doing well. Even though we may not always say the right things, they are thankful for our attempts to make them smile.

ASKING FOR HELP FROM ADULTS

Some kids go to adults, such as parents, teachers, or pastors, to deal with friends who have problems. We think that these adults know how to help more than us. We assume that they can help us understand the situation and figure out how to support our friends. But this can lead to tension between the one who is trying to help and the one who is hurting.

I have a good friend, whom I will refer to as Jacob, who talked to me about this experience: He was severely depressed and had thoughts of suicide. He told his best friend, whom I will refer to as Matthew, about it. Matthew didn't know what to do to help Jacob, so he shared Jacob's experience with a church leader. This leader then discussed the issue with Jacob. My friend told me, "He made it worse since he was just telling me what to do, like get over yourself, and when you say that to a depressed kid, it just adds on." Jacob was more depressed after this conversation. Jacob continued to tell me, "I realized that Matthew was just trying to help, but I'd rather go for help myself than have him try to get help for me, because that's pretty much unnecessary conflict with others that I wanna avoid." Jacob felt that his best friend had let him down, causing him to feel "lonely and betrayed."

It is better to wait until the friend who is troubled is ready to speak to an adult instead of talking for him. But sometimes, if the friend is really hurting and we're scared for him, then we might ask our friend for permission to talk to an adult to help him.

KNOWING WHAT TO DO WHEN

Adolescents cope with friends' distress by listening and being there for them. From Yumi's own experiences as well as from the data gathered, it appears to be that kids tend not to give advice when friends are troubled. They seem to know, unlike many adults, that telling people what to do rarely helps in situations where there are no easy, formulaic answers.

When a friend is worried about her driving test, and your teen has already taken and passed it, it is helpful to share what was on the test. However, when a friend is angry and anxious, because he had a fight with his dad about not working hard enough to make the club soccer team, it is usually not beneficial to give your opinion about what he should have done and what he needs to do now. Most people, particularly kids who are highly agitated at that moment, are not ready to hear this yet, and thus, cannot assimilate this information in any constructive way.

This way of "helping" may result in the one who gives advice to feel superior and self-righteous, and the one receiving the input to feel even more inadequate and upset. Words and actions that convey the feeling of being heard is the most valuable gift to offer someone in distress.

ROLE OF EMPATHY

When we are someone's friend, it is a responsibility and a privilege to be able to hear her suffering, be supportive, and walk with her through her experience. When our teenagers are in distress, we would want this for them from their friends. It is essential for character and moral development to allow our teens to also care for the well-being of their friends through listening and providing encouragement.

This requires empathy, a capacity to recognize and understand the emotional experience of another within the other's frame of reference. This kind of compassion – choosing to step in the other person's "shoes" to share the other's feelings and thoughts – is necessary for relationships to thrive. It is vital to raise our children to be empathic.

On the other hand, it is this capacity for empathy that concerns parents when their teens are dealing with distressed friends: Their teens may be negatively influenced by their friends who are troubled. Many studies have found that when we empathize, there are changes that occur within us neurologically, emotionally, and physically.[8,9]

The more attuned we are to another, i.e., the more empathic we are, the more we are impacted internally as a result of that connection. Listening to someone else's emotions stimulates our own brain regions that are involved in experiencing similar emotions. It is as if we are actually going through what we are observing in the other.

What this means is that when empathic teens are faced with a distressed friend, they will also mimic that distress in their brains and mirror the emotions they perceive. This then helps the ones listening to be able to truly understand what their friend is going through, and because of this, their friend will feel heard and validated. This leads to their friend feeling lighter for having shared. However, it may leave the ones listening feeling more burdened for a time.

There are certain situations where a friend's crisis surpasses our teens' ability to understand and cope, whether or not they realize and accept this as fact. In these circumstances, it is important to consider our kids' susceptibility to distress and resilience in the face of adversity.

BALANCE BETWEEN SELF-CARE AND OTHER-CARE

There is a delicate balance between taking care of others who are hurting and protecting oneself from being depleted or overwhelmed. If an adolescent is vulnerable to undue influence from peers and/or demonstrates risk factors delineated in the previous chapter, then it is even more imperative to explore where to draw the boundary between helping someone else and taking care of himself.

An example of a situation that occurs in the teen world, especially among girls, involves self-injurious behaviors which have been increasing in the recent years.[10] These include cutting, scratching, burning, and carving of the skin as well as swallowing toxic substances and pulling out one's hair. It is not unusual for certain teenagers to engage in self-mutilation when they are experiencing emotional pain.

The average teen will not know how to understand why his friend is doing this nor to help her stop. If someone is doing this, and tells a friend how much better she feels afterward, a teen who is relatively healthy, might find this really confusing and bizarre. On the other hand, if a teen who is at risk for various mental health issues hears this, she might be more inclined to try this method of feeling better as well. Instead of being a positive resource for her friend, she has now joined her in using maladaptive means of managing distress.

HOW RESILIENT ARE OUR CHILDREN?

Another factor to consider as we help our children cope with their friends' pain is to examine our kids' hardiness. Psychological resilience refers to people's capacity to withstand and adaptively manage stressful events.[11] Resilient teens are protected from negative outcomes and are able to recover relatively fast from traumas.

They are also more inclined to use painful experiences to learn and grow, which furthers their ability to "bounce back" from hurtful events in the future. These children will most likely be strong enough to provide support and assistance to their troubled peers without feeling overwhelmed by them.

When a teenager is not resilient, it is important to be more careful about exposing him to significant stressors since he will be more negatively affected by them. However, life, especially in the teen world, is filled with angst. In addition, we would want our children to be caring of others, which means that they need to learn to listen and be available to their friends. Thus, rather than having them avoid stressful situations, it is more valuable to develop hardiness in our kids.

Factors that have been associated with resilience[12] include:

- a stable relationship with at least one caring adult
- spiritual foundation which gives a sense of meaning and purpose
- realistic expectations and high support to meet them
- warm, nurturing, and respectful family environment
- emotional intelligence, i.e., the ability to perceive, use, understand, and manage emotions.

As an added note, an adolescent who has the above characteristics (e.g., a close relationship with his parents) is less likely to be influenced by his peers to engage in high-risk behaviors.[13]

Teenagers can also read about how to develop resilience in themselves in the American Psychological Association's article, *10 Tips to Build Resilience,* on its website.[14] In essence, being connected to a support system; caring about something more than oneself; taking time to engage in behaviors that reinforce physical, mental, and spiritual health; and feeling free to express oneself are various ways to increase inner strength. When our children are resilient, they are more likely to take care of themselves and others well.

REFLECTIONS

A. Have you ever worried about your teens' friends?

    If yes, why? _____

    _____

B. Are there certain friends in particular that you are concerned about?

    If yes, who? _____

    _____

C. Do you think that your teens can handle various issues that may come up with their friends?

    If yes, why? _____

    _____

    If no, why not? _____

    _____

D. My teenagers have the following risk factors:

    ☐ Predisposition to Mental Health Issues*

    ☐ No Sense of Meaning and Purpose

    ☐ Low Self-Esteem

    ☐ Abusive, Negligent Family Relationships

    ☐ Lack of Emotional Intelligence

      *Check this if you endorsed any of the warning signs listed in chapter 3, and if there is a family history of mental illnesses, and/or if your teens have experienced any trauma(s).

E. My kids have the following factors associated with resilience:

☐ Stable, Caring Relationship With At Least One Adult

☐ Spiritual Beliefs and Practices

☐ Realistic Expectations and High Support to Meet Them

☐ Positive Family Environment

☐ Emotional Intelligence

F. Write down ideas you have to increase your teens' resilience in the specific categories described above (e.g., encouraging children to identify and express their feelings will help to build their emotional intelligence):

_____

_____

_____

FROM KNOWLEDGE TO ACTION

A. The importance of facilitating resilience in your teenagers cannot be overstated. The factors listed above are some ways in which you can inoculate your teens from negative influences, outcomes, and disorders.

B. Depending on where your teens fall on the "risk–resilience continuum," you can decide how much to intervene when they are dealing with friends who are in distress. When they are not feeling or doing well, they will find it more challenging to be wise about what to do in these situations. Take the time to explain how important their well-being is to you and how it can be negatively affected by their choice in friends and their issues. Affirm their desire to be a good friend while also impressing upon them the need for protection from harm.

C. It is our responsibility as parents to gauge the emotional, mental, and relational health of our teenagers and guide them to make choices that reflect a balance of caring for themselves as well as others.

D. On occasion, our children may approach us with their concerns regarding a friend's difficult situation and ask us to not say anything to his parents. I have told my kids that I am happy to listen to anything they would like to share, but that I cannot keep confidential any information that I determine would put that child or others at risk of being seriously injured in some way. However, before I say anything to anyone, I give my children a chance to talk to their friends into sharing their problems with their parents or another adult that they trust first.

E. Please review with your teens what you believe they and their friends can handle on their own: Situations that do not call for your intervention. It is also important to clarify what kinds of circumstances require you to share what you know with other parents in order to ensure the safety of the teens involved.

   1. Some examples of situations that do not mandate adult intervention:

      (a) Friend Drama, e.g., there is hurt, because one friend is talking about another behind her back.

(b) Academic Stress, e.g., there is anxiety due to falling grades.

(c) Extra-curricular Pressure, e.g., there is resentment, because the coach did not play him as much as another teammate who is worse than he is.

(d) Parent Conflicts, e.g., there is anger, because his dad grounded him from playing video games until his grades improve.

2. Some examples of situations that necessitate adult intervention:

(a) A friend who has been depressed and is now talking about suicide.

(b) A friend who is engaging in self-injurious behaviors.

(c) A friend who is drinking and driving.

(d) A friend who is having unprotected sex.

F. Invite your teens to talk with you if they are concerned about any of their friends so that you can help them explore how best to walk alongside their troubled friends. This also gives you an opportunity to become aware of your own kid's thoughts and feelings.

Chapter 5

Expressing Individuality

*What is the appeal of all
the body "art" including writings,
piercings, and tattoos?*

*H*ave you noticed that more and more adolescents seem to have multiple piercings and tattoos? I was in Starbuck's the other day where I was being served by an older teen with studs on her eyebrow, tongue, and of course, her ears. I hurt just looking at her. Next to her was a young man with a very large, colorful tattoo all over his left arm as well as with a gauge (a.k.a. tunnel, earlet, plug) on his ear lobes so big that I could probably fit a quarter through it. I found myself wincing and could not look at him either.

I am cringing even as I recall these images. Perhaps I am too old-fashioned and traditional, or maybe they have strange ideas about beauty. Even as I shrink away from the imagined pain and the unattractiveness (in my opinion) of these sorts of body art, I am also fascinated by how they look.

I have noticed that some younger teens who have not yet ventured into getting tattoos and/or piercings in various body parts are writing/drawing on themselves. Is this a prelude of things to come? Yumi got her ear lobes pierced when she was around 12 years old. A couple of years later, she asked if she can have more perforations in her ear lobes. I thought one pair of holes was enough. She fought to have more.

Now, my 15-year-old son is flirting with the idea of getting his ear lobes pierced. Although I am not rigidly opposed to his desire to do this, I am in the process of persuading him that this is not the best look for him. I can see the beauty in some of the piercings and tattoos, but I find it difficult to appreciate why kids would pierce and tattoo themselves on multiple areas of their bodies in assorted ways.

BODY ART LOOKS GOOD

*M*any, not all, find body art appealing. Some teens like the way it looks. I won the argument with my mom: I have double piercings on both ears and a piercing on the top ridge of my right ear. I saw others with these kinds of piercings, and I thought they looked good. So, I got them. Many kids talk about how "cute," "pretty," "sexy," "stylish" and "cool" body art can be. Obviously, "beauty is in the eye of the beholder."

A WAY TO BE NOTICED

Others use body art to be noticed. Some kids are really into being the center of attention. They use their piercings and tattoos to get attention from others. Teenagers typically have piercings on their ears, lips, nose, eyebrows, and belly buttons. Some teens have tattoos on their arms, backs, shoulders, and behind their ears. The more body art one has, the more likely he is to draw attention to himself.

"IT'S MY BODY!"

Most teens get piercings and tattoos as a form of rebellion. Many parents do not approve of body art. They may be fine with single ear piercings. But, after that, no more is allowed. So, teens go behind their parents' backs to get it done, and then hide it for as long as possible underneath their clothes or hair. Eventually, they have to face the wrath of their parents. But by then, it's too late to undo it. Body art is a way of saying, "It's my body, and I can do what I want!" Our bodies belong to us, not our parents. They run our lives in most areas, but in this, we should be able to have some control.

EXPRESSING OURSELVES

Many kids use body art as a way to express themselves. It's a way to convey our thoughts, feelings, and beliefs. As Melissa (16-year-old junior) states, "body art, in my opinion, is just another way to set yourself apart from everyone else – a way to be 'original.' " I have a friend who wants to get a tattoo of a phrase in a foreign language on her back. This phrase stands for how she wants to live her life. She hasn't seen anyone with this exact tattoo and finds it unique. It's an expression of who she is.

If I were to get a tattoo, I would choose to ink Philippians 4:6.[15] This is a Bible verse that helps me to not be anxious and instead trust God to take care of me. I think it would remind me to relax each time I were to see this tattoo on my hand.

ORIGINS OF BODY ART

Tattooing and piercings date back to the ancient times throughout the world. Many cultures have used piercings and tattoos to commemorate a significant event, as a rite of passage, as a part of a spiritual ritual, to enhance sexual pleasure, to symbolize status, and for aesthetic reasons. For example, nose piercings with bones and feathers were popular among the tribes of New Guinea to denote wealth and virility among men.

However, there are also cultures and religions that have prohibited these practices. Some passages of the Bible[16] have been interpreted as forbidding any tattoos or piercings, which have led certain Christians to eschew these behaviors. The Old Testament and other religious texts are also used in Judaism to prohibit its people from defacing their bodies via tattoos and piercings.

Each generation seems to choose different manifestations of the unconventional to explore its identity, differentiate from previous mores, and make a certain statement through a particular fashion. Adolescents who are open to new experiences and drawn to experimenting with new styles are more likely to be part of the group who is able to see beauty in the unusual or different.

The more traditional and conservative members of a generation might be more inclined to see these as being "weird" and "ugly." The pull of this latter group may make this current trend of body piercing and tattooing a fad that will pass sooner or later. In the meantime, parents will hear "everyone is doing it" as a refrain from their teens when arguing for their rights to pierce and ink their bodies.

BODY ART: AN EXPRESSION OF THE SELF

In today's youth culture, it is not uncommon to see these types of body art, even though it is illegal in most states for anyone under 18 years old to get a tattoo. Surveys suggest that approximately 23% of teens have body piercings (in places other than ear lobes) while 8% have tattoos.[17] Yumi mentions that many adolescents like these and want them, because they look good, command attention, demonstrate rebellion, and express individuality.

These motives are important considerations in the development of one's identity. Adolescents' sense of self is informed by how they appear and whether they draw positive or negative interest from others. It is also dependent upon how successfully they navigate the "separation-individuation" stage of development.

This refers to a process where toddlers begin to conceptualize how they are separate entities from their parents. They begin to discover their own thoughts and feelings, and to express these in no uncertain terms. At this time, life becomes more about figuring out their boundaries, e.g., what is mine and what is yours. Mostly, it is about "me, myself, and I."

This phase of egocentrism also occurs in adolescence. As teens experience further differentiation of self from others, especially parents, they begin to consolidate an understanding of who they are within and who they are in relationship to their world. Rebelling against parental constraints is a universal method of trying to distinguish who they are from their parents. It is a way of exploring differing values, beliefs, and styles to see what fits with who they think they are and who they want to be.

Piercings and tattoos are one way of manifesting differentiation from their parents, peers, and/or cultural norms. Thus, the battle cry, "It is my body! I can do what I want." More teens are engaging in these types of body art today than ever before.

CORRELATION BETWEEN BODY ART AND OTHER TEEN BEHAVIORS

While these practices of body piercing and tattooing are no longer the purview of people on the fringes of society, they are not the majority either. Multiple studies indicate that adolescents who pierce and tattoo their bodies are more likely to have engaged in risk-taking behaviors, such as, fighting, smoking, using drugs, and having sex.[18] The younger the age at the time of tattooing and body piercing, the more possibility of substance use and suicide.

Surveys also indicate that body art is more common in girls than boys. This may be due to the historical trends of girls accessorizing themselves more than boys. Given the disquieting statistics above, it is essential to know and understand our teens' propensity to test the boundaries. Some amount of pushing is normal; however, when this is joined by other risk-taking behaviors, it is important to intervene to keep our kids healthy and safe.

REFLECTIONS

A. Do your teenagers have any piercings? Yes ☐ No ☐

   If yes, how many? ____ Where? _____

   _____

B. Do you have any piercings? Yes ☐ No ☐

   If yes, how many? ____ Where? _____

   _____

   List your reasons for getting them: _____

   _____

C. Do your teens have any tattoos? Yes ☐ No ☐

   If yes, how many? ____ Where? _____

   _____

D. Do you have any tattoos? Yes ☐ No☐

   If yes, how many? ____ Where? _____

   _____

   List your reasons for getting them: _____

   _____

E. Do your teens have any close friends who have piercings and/or tattoos? Yes ☐ No ☐

   If yes, how many close friends? ____ Where? _____

   _____

F. Have your teens approached you about having more piercings or tattoos? Yes ☐ No ☐

If yes, how did you respond? _____

_____

Why did you respond this way? _____

_____

If you are asked in the future, how do you plan to respond?

_____

_____

FROM KNOWLEDGE TO ACTION

A. If your teens are asking for body piercings and tattoos, it is important to have discussions about their requests.

1. If you are opposed to them getting it, just saying, "No! Over my dead body!" usually leads to them wanting it even more and perhaps doing it without your permission.

   (a) Listen to their reasons.

   (b) Demonstrate your understanding of how they want to be like their "cool" peers who have them, how they want to exert ownership over their body by having a choice to do this, and/or how they find them to be beautiful.

   (c) Once your teenagers feel heard, then they will be in a better place to listen to you.

   • Communicate your concerns about these types of body art due to the studies that show a correlation between adolescent body piercings and tattoos with risk-taking behaviors.

   • Discuss their reasons for wanting it. If these are similar to those of other teenagers depicted in this chapter, explore other ways of looking good, getting attention, asserting independence, and expressing themselves.

   • Ask them to think about future implications. For all intents and purposes, tattoos are permanent. Usually, piercings leave holes even when you stop putting jewelry in them.

   • How would they enjoy having these during their 40s, 60s, 80s? Will the design or style still be something that is considered to be attractive, "cool," makes a statement about who they are, throughout the years of their lives? Will they project the kind of image they want as they look for specific jobs? As they seek marriage partners?

   • Talk to them about costs. Tattoos can be expensive. Piercings also can be expensive when you bear in mind all the jewelry you need to have to fill the holes over a lifetime.

2. If you are open to them getting it, consider doing the following (some of which are the same as above):

(a) Listen to their reasons.

(b) Validate them.

(c) Encourage them to think about the link between risk-taking behaviors and body piercings and tattoos.

(d) If they are considering getting a particular design that is sexual or violent in nature or getting piercings/tattoos on private body parts, ask them to think about the implications. For example, tattoos on the lower back are called, "tramp stamps." Is this how they want to be known? There is also greater danger in having nipple piercings: They have been correlated with breast abscesses.

(e) Establish guidelines:

• where your teens can have it done

• what part of the body is permissible for them to pierce or tattoo

• what images are acceptable/unacceptable to ink on the body

• what types of "jewelry" are acceptable/unacceptable to put into the piercings.

B. There are health risks to getting body piercing and tattoos. If done improperly, they can lead to infections such as hepatitis and blood-borne diseases such as HIV. It is essential to talk with your teens about these risks and how to prevent them. For example, piercing needles should be sterilized and should not be shared.

C. As mentioned earlier, most states have an age requirement of 18 or older to get a tattoo. Some disreputable tattoo parlors will do the job on minors in spite of this law. Thus, it is advisable to find those that belong to a professional body art association, because they are more likely to follow standard guidelines that lessen the risk of health problems.

Chapter 6

Dressing for Peer Success

Why are the bottoms so high and tops so low for girls? Why are the bottoms so low for boys?

When you see teen girls, do you ever have an urge to tell them to wear longer skirts/shorts and higher-necked tank tops/t-shirts? When I see girls, especially in the winter, wearing clothes that are really low-cut and short, I want to cover them up. Not only are their body parts exposed to the public, but they also look cold. Perhaps I'm projecting my own discomfort onto these kids. Sometimes, Yumi dresses in multiple layers – tank top, t-shirt, sweater, and a jacket – because she is cold, but her neck and upper chest area are bare (all the layers are low-cut). It seems to me that she would still be cold due to leaving these areas uncovered.

How about when you see teen boys? Do you ever notice how boys wear their pants lower than they are supposed to with the bottom edges pooling around their ankles? I want to tell them to pull up their jeans. How could it be comfortable to have their pants' waist be in the middle of their hips? I know I would worry about my slacks falling down if I were to wear them this way. Of course, I would look and feel ridiculous too.

I know that not all teenagers dress this way. However, it seems to be the majority that do. What about those kids that do not follow this trend? If your teenager is one of these teens that dress the way we, as adults, would like, have you wondered why they do not wear their clothes like their peers?

Perhaps they are more self-assured, do not care about what peers think/do, have not yet clued in to the current fashion styles, and/or are more attached to their parents' views of what is appropriate. For those girls who are dressing in shorts/skirts too short and tops too low, and for those boys who are wearing their pants too low, what are the reasons for their choices?

BEING JUDGED

Teens often judge people by what they see. Girls dress in low-cut shirts and short shorts/skirts, while boys sag their pants, because they think these styles are chic. They dress like this to look good for others. Sometimes, kids don't want to be associated with those whose outward appearances are unappealing. It's not right, but it's true. Those who dress poorly are criticized. If a guy is wearing pants that are too short and pulled up to his waist, then he is made fun of. No one wants to hang out with kids like him. So, it's important to dress "cool" and "hot" in order to be accepted.

INFLUENCE OF MEDIA

Media often influences teens' ideas about what is attractive. Most of us think what is attractive is sexy. Everyone wants to follow the fashion trends that they see models and actors wearing. Andy (16-year-old junior) states, "Media makes girls believe more skin is more appealing." By revealing more of themselves – boys with showing off their boxers and girls with showing off their chest and legs – they are hoping to look desirable.

Teens tend to dress in clothes that they see others wearing, because they feel insecure about themselves. If we dress like the people we see in magazines and movies, then we feel more popular and beautiful. We think we fit in better.

KNOWING WHAT LOOKS GOOD

Kids choose to wear these types of clothing sometimes, because they're the most flattering look for them. For example, one of the teens surveyed shared that she has short legs and wearing short skirts makes her legs look longer.

Another teen states that he sags to hide his butt since he doesn't think that he has a nice one. So, some of us choose to dress the way we do, because we know the look that is best for us. And we feel comfortable when we think that we look good.

SIGNIFICANCE OF PHYSICAL APPEARANCE

Physical appearance is important to most of us. The way we look includes physiological characteristics (e.g., height, weight, body shape, skin color) as well as what we wear. We might not be able to change the way we are in the physical realm. However, we do have some control over what we wear, and thus, how we express who we are through our dress. By our choices in clothing, we can manifest a certain image, have an illusion of change in our physical traits, and feel more or less confident.

Our physical presentation then is evaluated by those around us in obvious and subtle ways. Some of us, more than others, may internalize this feedback as being real and true of us. Thus, how we choose to reveal ourselves through our dress has ramifications for who we are and how we feel about ourselves.

This is especially true of teens. Physical appearance is extremely significant during adolescence. Teenagers spend hours contemplating and experimenting with different styles to find that perfect balance between fitting in and standing out (in a "cool" way). While teens do make remarks about their own and others' physiological traits, they are more likely to make judgmental comments about what others are wearing. Clothing is a part of a teen's look that defines her.

Teens are given input – directly and indirectly – about how they look. When they wear the "wrong" labels, styles, and designs, there are observations that are made not just about the clothes per se but also about the person. She may be labeled a "nerd" or a "slut." This then becomes internalized as being a part of who she is, particularly if she is more vulnerable to others' thoughts about her.

Depending on how she is dressed, she may be admired and accepted or ridiculed and rejected by her peers. This can contribute to an increase or decrease in her sense of self-worth.

Not only a teenager's clothing, but how he accessorizes, also makes an impact on his own sense of self and how others see him. The kind of shoes, the type of hats, the sort of jewelry, and even the style of socks affect how he feels about himself, much of which is informed by how others think about his appearance.

Of course, this is even more so for teen girls than boys since they have a greater variety of accessories and looks to choose from. Many adolescents look alike from head to toe due to shopping in the same stores to project the same image.

DRESSING TO BE LIKE EVERYONE ELSE

Unlike tattoos and piercings which seem to be more about expressing one's uniqueness, the ways in which teens dress seem to be more about being like everyone else. They emulate what they see in the media (e.g., tv, music videos, movies, magazines, video games, internet). Usually, the societal messages in these mediums tend to be a standard of beauty that is rather narrow and unrealistic. There is uniformity in what media portrays as being attractive and sexy.

Parents are not immune to this pressure to conform either and may be reinforcing this model in their own attire. Thus, it is not surprising that many kids are wearing the same things, i.e., the current trend of revealing and tight clothes for girls, and loose and sagging clothes for boys.

For some of the kids, this may just be a matter of clothing preference that may have negligible relevance to self-esteem issues. As Yumi points out, the choice to wear certain types of clothes may have more to do with what teens feel comfortable in and what they think looks good on them rather than pleasing others. However, for many of the kids, these types of clothing may be closely related to their levels of self-acceptance and self-respect.

"SELF-OBJECTIFICATION"

Psychologists have identified "self-objectification" as a potential issue among teens, particularly girls, who dress in a sexualized fashion.[19] This theoretical concept refers to viewing one's own body as an object of others' desires. Those who dress to look "sexy" are more likely to objectify themselves.

In self-objectification, people learn to consider themselves as objects to be gazed at and appraised for their appearance. Some individuals may think and feel this way consistently and not be able to fully engage with who they are as a whole person with talents, interests, and capabilities. This can lead to cognitive and emotional difficulties.

Researchers[20] conducted an experiment in which they asked college students to wear either a swimsuit or a sweater and evaluate the clothing by looking into a full-length mirror. They were then asked to complete an advanced math test. They found that young women who were dressed in the swimsuit performed significantly worse than those wearing sweaters.

The researchers concluded that wearing the swimsuit prompted a sense of being on display, increased consciousness about one's appearance, and feelings of shame triggered from comparisons between one's body with the cultural ideal. These thoughts and feelings disrupted their performances.

Mental resources were drawn away from the test and channeled into other areas that impaired their cognitive functioning. Subsequent studies[21] have confirmed that self-objectifying situations cause negative cognitive and emotional outcomes for men as well as for various ethnic groups.

What are the implications of these studies for our teenagers who dress in a more sexualized fashion? For many kids, particularly those who are insecure and vulnerable, this may mean that they think and feel like objects to be evaluated and used for others' pleasure. This way of looking at themselves is correlated with a self-image that is formed by societal messages that place a much greater value on the outer appearance rather than on inner character and abilities.

This obviously can cause a damaged sense of self: (a) Cognitive deficits in which they may not be able to learn and/or perform well on mentally challenging tasks; (b) Emotional difficulties which may include body image issues, eating disorders, anxiety, and depression; and (c) Relational challenges in which adolescents' impaired perceptions of themselves interfere with their ability to relate to others in healthy ways.

REFLECTIONS

A. How do your teenagers dress? _____

_____

B. What kinds of images do you try to project with your clothing?

_____

C. What messages are you giving to your kids by the way you dress?

_____

D. Are you satisfied with the way your teens look? Yes ☐ No☐

   If yes, what do you like about it? _____

   If no, what bothers you? _____

E. Do your kids wear clothes that are similar/different than their peers?

   Similar ☐ Different ☐

   What does this mean for your teens and for you?

_____

F. Do you struggle with concerns about physical appearance? Yes ☐ No ☐

   If yes, in what ways? _____

_____

G. Do you talk about your own and others' struggles with outward appearances (e.g., "Do I look fat?" "I need to be on a diet." "She dresses like a teenager.")? Yes ☐ No ☐

   If yes, how? _____

_____

H. Do you self-objectify? Yes ☐ No ☐

   In what ways? _____

   _____

I. Do you observe any self-objectification in your kids? Yes ☐ No ☐

   In what ways? _____

   _____

FROM KNOWLEDGE TO ACTION

A. <u>Ask</u> your teens about how they dress and <u>listen</u> to what they have to say:

   1. What do they like about the way they look?

   2. Why do they wear the clothes the way they do?

   3. Are they aware of sending certain messages by their choices in clothing?

   4. How do they feel about their friends' (here you might name a few) attire?

B. Discuss with your teens the concept of self-objectification. To reiterate, it is treating their bodies as objects to be displayed and evaluated by others. It is a third-person view of themselves rather than a first-person position in which they can experience all of who they are.

C. You might try an experiment to underscore how self-objectification works.

   1. Ask your teenagers for about 30 minutes of their time. Do not tell your kids what this experiment is about: You will contaminate the results if you do. Place them in a quiet room where they can be by themselves when they are performing the task.

   2. Request your teens to do an assignment (e.g., writing an essay, doing a math test from textbooks/SAT study books, or figuring out a Sudoku puzzle) when you notice that they happen to be wearing t-shirt/sweater and pants/jeans (i.e., their bodies are covered more than not).

   3. Give them 15 minutes to complete the task.

   4. When they are done, ask about any thoughts/feelings they might have had while doing the work. Write these down.

   5. Then have your teens dress in a swimsuit, take a look at themselves in the mirror for a few minutes, and then do another

complicated task – same type and level of difficulty as before (really important!).

6. After 15 minutes, ask them what thoughts/feelings surfaced during the task. Write these down.

7. Score both results. Compare the scores and their thoughts/ feelings during the two testing situations.

8. Are there any similarities or differences between the two situations? Discuss the meaning and implications of this experiment with your teens.

D. If your teenagers' self-worth is linked too much with how others think of their physical appearances, it is essential to do the following:

1. Consider how you might have modeled and reinforced this behavior by your words and behaviors.

    (a) What kinds of clothes do you buy for yourself and others in the family?

    (b) Do you consistently make comments about how you or others look?

    (c) Are you constantly on a diet?

2. Discuss with them the damaging effects of being sexualized and objectified. People who self-objectify are more likely to:

    (a) be comfortable with being used by others

    (b) feel anxious, ashamed, and/or depressed

    (c) have eating and weight management issues

    (d) experience lack of self-respect, self-acceptance, and self-worth.

3. Emphasize the significance of basing their self-image on the internal self: talents, interests, strengths, areas for growth.

E. One last thought: Just because your kids are dressing to fit with the current trends does not mean that they will have mental health issues. It is important to take into account the degree to which they rely on physical appearance to give them a sense of worth, the severity of self-objectification, and other variables, such as quality of their family and peer relationships.

Chapter 7

Making Choices

What makes a teen choose to lie,
cheat, drink, use drugs, and/or have sex?

When we hear about a teenager whose life has derailed into lying, cheating, alcohol, drugs, and/or sex, we live in the comfort of our denial that our teens would not engage in these sorts of behaviors. It is always someone else's child who is like this. It would be nice to bypass parenting woes by having our children emerge from adolescence unscathed by these potentially disturbing issues.

Actually, given the "right" set of circumstances, any teen can fall into these paths. Certainly, what teen has not lied or cheated at something, sometime? Not as many perhaps have engaged in drinking, using drugs, and/or having sex. Nonetheless, these also seem to be prevalent among the current teens.

Do you remember the movie, Freaky Friday (2003)? The mom, performed by Jamie Lee Curtis, advises her teenage daughter, played by Lindsay Lohan, to "make good choices" as she drops her off at school while the daughter rolls her eyes at her mom.

I have been known to say this exact thing as I drop my kids off at school, mall, friends' houses, etc. It makes me feel better to remind them once more to do what is right as I allow them to go into their own world. I doubt that my last minute prompt to my kids as they are getting out of the car really makes a difference to them. They probably will do what they have learned thus far from their upbringing and as their need for differentiation at this stage leads them.

As parents, we want to help our kids make good choices. To this end, we need to have a better idea of what they are doing. Our kids will roll their eyes at us if we just lay down the law instead of understanding what they are about. How do we know when they get off the tracks? What can we do to prevent them from making bad choices? How should we respond to them if they do? Why do they make the decision to lie, cheat, drink, use drugs, and/or have sex?

DIFFICULT CHOICES

A lot of times teens choose to do things that they know are wrong. When they go through tough times, some teens do things like drugs to escape life. Others to be "cool," impress people, and fit in. Some do these things out of curiosity. Some teenagers also think these activities are "fun."

WAYS TO ESCAPE

Many kids in the survey said that they would make the choices above as an escape – from life, consequences, etc. My friend went through a painful time because of a girl, and used this as an excuse to start smoking. He didn't think that he would become addicted when he began, but he eventually did. This "heartbreak" happened almost three to four years ago, and he still smokes. He said smoking makes him feel better. It helps him forget about all the pain that he's going through. He has tried to quit many times, but he's been unsuccessful.

Teens drink and do drugs as a way of dealing with the pressures of life. These behaviors help them to "relax" and run away from their realities.

I've lied to my parents to avoid their disappointment and punishment. I can't think of a single friend who hasn't lied to their parents about something in order to get away with what they did (that was wrong).

One friend cheated on a test and got caught. She was worried that her parents would get mad if she got a bad grade on a test in that class. She didn't want to let her parents down, and so, she resorted to cheating to get a better grade. When she had to tell her parents, they were more upset with her decision to cheat than the grade. She tried to escape the consequences of not studying enough and getting the grade she deserved by cheating.

TO FIT IN

Many teenagers want to fit in: They want to be like others that they think are "cool." So, they drink, do drugs, and/or hook up at parties to feel like they are "chill" too.

I had a friend who was innocent and wholesome in middle school. When he became a freshman in high school, he started to hang out with a group of kids who partied a lot. He thought they were popular. He wanted to be like them. So he went to parties, and began drinking, doing drugs, and eventually having sex. He now has a reputation for being "hot" in some groups, while being "stupid" in others.

SATISFY CURIOSITY

Some kids are curious about what it's like to have alcohol, do drugs, and sleep around. They're often influenced by older siblings, parents, and friends who do these things.

My friend, whom I will call Elizabeth, has an older sister who likes to drink at home. Because Elizabeth was around her and other family members who would frequently drink, she began to wonder what it was about alcohol that people seem to like so much. She started drinking when she was in middle school. She has talked about the different drinks her sister has made and how "good" they are. She started drinking out of curiosity but ended up getting hooked, because she found alcohol "yummy."

HAVING FUN

Many teens who do these behaviors find them "fun." In the case of lying and cheating, these kids may feel a nervous rush in the middle of anticipating and doing these things, but afterward, when they get away with whatever they're doing, they feel relieved and happy.

When people are high on drugs, they look like they're having fun. And they've told me that they feel free and elated. It's funny to watch them lose control and do things that they wouldn't normally do.

One time, a student came into class high. It was clear that he was on drugs because of the way his eyes looked and his actions. He started playing with the classroom's hand sanitizer. He was swishing it around and making "ooo" and "ahh" noises. He was fascinated by the hand sanitizer. At the moment he was amused, but when he was sober and realized what he had done, he was embarrassed.

I guess if we really think through our choices and their end results, we might make smarter decisions. I think it's hard for teens to really think of how our present actions will affect our future since our future seems so far away.

SHORT-TERM VS. LONG-TERM VIEW

Time is elongated when young. It is only when we are older that we realize how fast time flies and how our future has now become our present. To most children, the future does not feel as relevant or real in comparison to the present. Thus, it is understandable that they make poor choices in the moment of life's stressors and peer pressures, among other variables.

However, not all succumb to behaviors such as lying, cheating, drinking, using illicit substances, and/or having sex. In order to further comprehend how these behaviors can become a part of your teen's world, it is helpful to be aware of the prevalence rates and risk factors. In addition, it is important to consider the physical and emotional manifestations of these choices in our teenagers.

PREVALENCE OF LYING AND CHEATING

When adolescents were surveyed about their honesty,[22] 42% said that they had lied to save some money, 83% said that they had lied to their parents, and 64% said they had cheated on a test in school within the past 12 months. In addition, 26% admitted to lying on the survey!

One would assume that they were lying to look better, and thus, the actual percentage of adolescents who had lied and cheated may be higher than what was indicated. What is more interesting and staggering than these percentages is that 93% of these adolescents said that they were content with their level of ethics and character.

Because so many of their peers lie and/or cheat, teens do not judge these behaviors as wrong. They are inured to them. Instead, these behaviors become part of the standard by which they measure integrity. Because these may be considered normative behaviors, it is difficult to observe any specific signs of lying and cheating when they occur.

If symptoms do manifest, depending on your child, you may notice guilty expressions, inability to look into your eyes when speaking, and fidgeting. It is interesting to note that when they do something wrong, some kids (like adults) may go on the offensive and behave with more irritability, annoyance, and defensiveness.

PREVALENCE OF ALCOHOL CONSUMPTION

In terms of alcohol use, researchers at University of Michigan recently conducted a survey in which they found that 37% of teens have consumed alcohol by eighth grade, and 72% have done so by the end of high school.[23] Underage drinking appears to be a relatively common experience for adolescents. As more peers drink, it feels less illegal and forbidden.

In fact, as with the previously mentioned behaviors of lying and cheating, there is a certain level of acceptance and, perhaps even approval, for consuming alcohol among adolescents. This parallels adult societal norms.

In 2008, Substance Abuse and Mental Health Services Administration (SAMHSA)[24] reported that the last time they had alcohol, 56% of youths ages 12-20 consumed alcohol in someone else's home, while 30% drank in their own home. Among this group, 31% paid for the alcohol, while 22% asked someone else to purchase it. Sometimes, adult family members provided the alcohol to the minor. If alcohol is readily available (due to having alcohol in the home or a person of legal age procuring it for the underage drinker), it is harder for teens to resist consuming it.

Other factors that increase the probability of drinking include low levels of parental supervision, family history of alcohol problems, impulse control issues, and thrill seeking behaviors. Those who have these risk factors may also increase their chances of being intoxicated and/or driving under the influence of alcohol. Alcohol inebriation is observable by the following: smell of alcohol on the teen's breath, glazed and/or bloodshot eyes, unsteady gait, and either undue passivity or belligerence.

PREVALENCE OF SUBSTANCE USE

SAMHSA also reports that from 2008 to 2009, 10% of youths ages 12-17 have used illegal drugs. The marijuana use rate among this age group is 7%. Their hallucinogen use is at 1%. Not as many adolescents engage in using substances like these in comparison to previously mentioned behaviors. Because of this, peer pressure is less, which then makes it easier for some to not begin this practice.

Illicit drugs are harder to acquire than alcohol. These are not found casually displayed or stored in homes the way that alcohol might be. The inaccessibility of illegal substances serves as a deterrent to those who might fall into using them.

However, teens can use/abuse legal "drugs," such as over-the-counter medications (e.g., Sudafed), prescription medications, and inhalants (e.g., gasoline) which are easily accessible. Any kind of substances can impair teens' ability to concentrate and make appropriate judgments. It increases their chances of engaging in sexual behaviors in addition to developing substance abuse issues in the future.

Risk factors for using illegal substances are similar to alcohol: Low levels of supervision, history of alcohol and drug use/abuse in the family, relational conflicts, and impulse control issues can increase the likelihood of engaging in this behavior. In addition, a history of physical and/or sexual abuse and emotional instability can contribute to a greater possibility of using drugs.

Effects of some types of drugs are manifested in the following ways: increased heart rate, dilated pupils, disorientation to time and space, volatile mood, memory loss, and perceptual distortions. These experiences may be pleasurable for some, while frightening for others.

PREVALENCE OF SEXUAL ACTIVITY

In 2009, according to the National Center for Chronic Disease Prevention and Health Promotion, 46% of high school students reported having had sexual intercourse (from 33% of 9th graders to 62% of 12th graders) and 14% had four or more sex partners during their teenage years.[25]

In another nationally representative survey, 24% of sexually active youths ages 15-17 reported feeling pressured to do something sexual that they did not really want to do and 21% stated having had oral sex to avoid sexual intercourse with a partner.[26] About 9% of high school students described having been physically forced to have sexual intercourse.

Teen girls with older male partners are more likely to be sexually active, less likely to use contraceptives, and more likely to face unintended pregnancies. Teen boys are significantly more likely than girls to initiate sexual intercourse. Urban youths are more likely than rural teens to engage in sexual activity. Prior to having sex, 22% of teens report consuming alcohol or drugs.

Other factors that increase the risk of engaging in sexual activity include the perception that "everyone is doing it," parental acceptance of early sexual behaviors, a history of physical or sexual abuse, and low levels of parental monitoring. Some of the signs that your teenager is sexually active might include presence of more secretive behaviors (especially about activities with their partners), desire to wash their own clothes, having items related to sexual activity (e.g., condoms), recurrent bladder infections, and symptoms of sexually transmitted diseases.

CAUSES FOR POOR CHOICES

It is really not surprising that a number of adolescents are feeling comfortable with lying, cheating, underage drinking, trying illegal drugs, and/or having sexual relations. Just consider the following variables cited by Yumi earlier:

- the reduced capacity for fully understanding future consequences of present choices
- feeling stressed and not having adaptive coping mechanisms
- experiencing peer pressure to be "cool" by engaging in these behaviors
- being curious about what it is like to do some of these activities
- wanting to have fun.

All of the above aspects (which are also part of normal

processes of development) combined with data on prevalence rates and risk factors make it clear how relatively easy it might be for teens to make poor choices.

As mentioned in an earlier chapter, a teen's brain has not fully matured yet. The section of the brain that facilitates judgment and planning is particularly underdeveloped. Thus, it may be challenging for teenagers to deliberate carefully and execute good decisions. This is one part of the picture. Other factors include stressors, peer pressures, one's inquisitiveness, and one's desires – all of which are part of life. Rather than trying to escape these, we need to teach our children how to manage these experiences more effectively.

REFLECTIONS

A. As far as you know, are your teens involved in any of the behaviors discussed above?

☐ Lying   ☐ Cheating   ☐ Drinking Alcohol

☐ Using Drugs   ☐ Having Sex

B. What are the signs that they are doing any of the above?

Mental (e.g., memory loss): _____

Emotional (e.g., more oppositional): _____

Physical (e.g., unsteady gait): _____

C. What are the risk factors in your teens' situation? The more variables you endorse, the more potential issues your teens may experience.

Risk Factors

Individual

Impulse Control Issues	☐ Yes	☐ No
Thrill Seeking Behaviors	☐ Yes	☐ No
Perception: "Everyone is Doing It"	☐ Yes	☐ No
Lack of Positive Coping Tools	☐ Yes	☐ No
History of Abuse	☐ Yes	☐ No

Family

Minimal Parental Supervision	☐ Yes	☐ No
Family History of Problems Re: Above Behaviors	☐ Yes	☐ No
Family Conflicts	☐ Yes	☐ No

Modeling by Older Siblings   ☐ Yes ☐ No

Community

Having Friends Who Engage in
These Behaviors   ☐ Yes ☐ No

Minimal Involvement in
Extra-Curricular Activities   ☐ Yes ☐ No

Peer Pressure   ☐ Yes ☐ No

Living in Urban Areas   ☐ Yes ☐ No

FROM KNOWLEDGE TO ACTION

A. We have examined some troubling teen behaviors, why some might choose these paths, and how parents can know when their kids derail. There are ways that you can prevent or intervene if your teens engage in these behaviors.

B. Some parents believe that talking about lying, cheating, drinking, drugs, and especially sex, will lead their teenagers to do these. Actually, one of the best protection against these behaviors is to converse with your teens about their potential exposure, choices, and consequences.

C. Conversations

    1. Set ground rules:

        (a) Let your teens know that you will not punish them for what they might say in this dialogue with you.

        (b) Emphasize the importance of honesty in this conversation.

        (c) Be clear with yourself in terms of your intentions as you pursue this communication:

            • to know your teens

            • to have influence in their lives

            • to set up future probability of them approaching you if/when these types of situations arise.

    2. Ask your teens the question we asked, "What makes a teen choose to lie, cheat, drink, use drugs, and/or have sex?"

        (a) Make sure you hear them first. Do not begin by telling them what you think.

        (b) Reflect their answers. Thus, you are letting them know that you heard what they said.

        (c) No matter what they tell you, do not express shock, judgment, or condemnation. The minute you do, they will most likely shut down.

(d) After you listen, share with them some of the things that teens have said in this chapter – some of which may or may not coincide with their views. You can also do this if your teenagers have difficulty responding to the initial question. This will help them get started in formulating their answers. Again, it is not you lecturing them about the subject, but saying, "I was reading this book, and in it, teens are saying that they are doing... because... What do you think?"

3. Follow-up with, "Have you ever lied, cheated, drank alcohol, used drugs, and/or had sex?"

(a) If they say yes, ask them for their reasons.

- Are they similar or different to the answers given in this chapter?

- Paraphrase what they say to you, again for the purpose of helping them to feel heard so that they continue to stay open to talking with you.

(b) If they say no, encourage them to share by prompting them:

- "I understand that the majority of kids lie, but you haven't?"

- "Lots of kids seem to cheat because they are anxious about getting bad grades and afraid of disappointing their parents: Can you relate to these kids?"

- "Drinking seems to be readily accepted by teens, but you don't have any desire to experiment?"

- "What helps you to stay away from illegal drugs?"

- "What is your personal boundary in terms of engaging in any kind of sexual activity?"

- After they answer your questions, make sure you take the time to consider their thoughts and feelings.

4. After listening, it is (finally!) your turn to express your opinion about what your teens have shared.

(a) Keep in mind the statistics presented earlier: Consider the data so that your expectations are reasonable.

(b) Remember that you want your teens to continue to talk with you so that you can have a positive impact in their lives.

(c) Do not make assumptions. For example, just because your teens are asking about a certain drug, it does not mean that they are thinking of or is currently using it.

(d) Use newspaper articles, television shows, movies, and real situations to make your point. Stories are much more interesting, and therefore better received, than lectures.

(e) Feel free to share your values. For example, if you believe in abstinence from sex prior to marriage, convey this truthfully and give reasons for this position.

(f) Brainstorm with your teens regarding ways to manage stress more effectively, to not be pressured by peers to abandon their own values, to assuage their curiosity, and to have fun in other ways.

(g) Review the risk factors table in the *Reflections* section, and figure out ways to reduce your teens' probability of engaging in these harmful behaviors.

(h) Most importantly, let your teens know that you welcome opportunities to talk with them about these matters always.

Chapter 8

Planting Seeds

*Do teens care about
their parents' opinions?*

When our children are young, we are their whole world. They cannot survive without us. They long to spend time with us. They listen to what we have to teach. They follow our directions. They even tell us and others how wonderful we are – at least until they begin school. I miss those days. How about you?

And then, they become teenagers. The demarcation between childhood, "tweens," and adolescence seems to be getting fuzzier and younger every year. Last year's child is this year's "tween," and last year's "tween" is this year's teen.

Once they become teenagers, they then talk and act as if they can live and even thrive without us. In fact, they prefer to spend time away from us. Not only do they not listen, they argue – a lot! They express to others how awful they think we are. One parent asked, "Why do my kids (who were 14 and 16 years old at the time) hate me?" It can sometimes feel like this.

No wonder many of us doubt that we matter to our teens. We are inundated with data that demonstrate how little they care: They invest more time and energy developing other relationships; We are told by the media that they care much more about what their friends think than what we believe; and They can be disrespectful, oppositional, and defiant with us. Does this mean that they do not consider our thoughts and feelings? Are our opinions irrelevant to them and their lives?

WE CARE

In our survey, about 62% of the teens stated that they care about their parents' opinions. Most of my friends and I are concerned with our parents' thoughts and feelings. In a previous chapter, I talked about how we like to keep our lives private from our parents. This is due to fear of being judged, disappointing our parents, and losing their trust. Obviously, it's because we care that we have these feelings.

SOMETIMES WE CARE

Approximately 30% expressed that depending on the situation, they may or may not be influenced by their parents' views. The kind of relationship that teenagers have with their parents makes a difference in their attitudes toward their parents' point of view. If teens have a strong relationship with their parents, they will be more open to listening to what their parents have to say. This is because these parents are also more interested in their teens' ideas.

Some revealed that they will pay attention to their parents if their parents say what they want to hear. One teen commented that if their parents express thoughts that they disagree with, then they "will disregard them." Other kids feel that they know more about what is going on than their parents; therefore, their parents' views are considered unimportant at times.

WE CAN'T ADMIT WE CARE

About 8% of the teens asserted that they don't care what their parents think or feel. I think that even these kids really do worry about pleasing their parents. They may be saying that they don't care, because maybe they're hurt and angry at their parents. I know teenagers like this. But the fact that they're upset illustrates that their parents' opinions do count.

Maybe some teens really don't care, because their parents don't care about them. Their parents may not love them and may even abuse them. In this case, teens are giving back to their parents what they've received.

STRONG CONNECTIONS
MAKE A DIFFERENCE

The above survey results are consistent with what is in the research literature. More often than not, adolescents are affected by their parents and do take the latter's thoughts and feelings into account. Whether they are dealing with relationships, pregnancy, sex, or substance use, teens endorse that their parents' opinions matter to them. The stronger the connection between parents and teens, the more likely they are to consider their parents' values and beliefs.

CONSCIOUS ADOPTION OF PARENTS' VIEWS

Adolescents are influenced by their parents in one of two ways. First, in specific areas of their lives, those with close relationships with their parents may consciously decide to adopt their parents' perspectives. On the other hand, those with distant or conflicted relationships with their parents may choose to reject their parents' views.

For example, in a positive relationship, when teenagers hear from their parents, "Do not get into a car with a driver who has been drinking," they will try to accept this as a legitimate position and apply it to their lives accordingly. This conscious consideration of parents' thoughts and feelings are not always clearly observable nor indicated to the parents. Nonetheless, it exists.

Imagine a situation where a parent is arguing with his teen regarding the merits of waiting to have sex until she is older. He asserts that she is not mature enough to make a decision regarding sex now. His teenager passionately disputes this and other opinions that he maintains. Later, he hears her disagreeing with a friend about the same issue, but this time, she is expressing his views as if they are her own. This dad may have been left with the impression that he was not heard earlier. However, in many of these situations, adolescents not only listened but are trying to utilize what they understood from their parents.

UNCONSCIOUS ASSIMILATION OF PARENTS' PERSPECTIVES

A second way in which parental influence occurs is through introjection, an unconscious assimilation of parental standards, ethics, and beliefs. This process is common to all children. As they develop, they absorb spoken and unspoken attitudes and behaviors that parents and the specific family environment espouse. They then follow or react against these outside of their awareness.

Yumi alludes to this process when she speaks about how even the kids who report that they do not care about their parents' opinions actually may be affected by their parents. Even as adolescents think that they are not shaped by their parents, at some level, they are being influenced.

For example, in a situation where a teen is exposed to a parent who is very organized and who demands this of the family members, this teen, depending on how he feels about his parent, may either adopt or refuse this way of being in the world. Whichever way he expresses this consciously, there is an unconscious level of making this a part of his identity: Either he becomes more comfortable in ordered and controlled environments or in the opposite, i.e., disordered and chaotic settings. Given his unconscious inclination, he will continue to create this as he develops his sense of self.

USING OUR INFLUENCES FOR GOOD

In any case, almost all adolescents are affected by their parents. Since they care about their parents' thoughts and feelings, it is important to discuss how best to use this knowledge to facilitate health in our teens. We titled this chapter, *Planting Seeds*. All that we say and do as parents is like "planting seeds."

There is a parable in the Bible (Book of Matthew, Chapter 13) about a farmer who scatters his seeds. The seeds drop into different places: some fall on the ground and fly away, others into rocky soil where they wither from lack of nutrients, yet others into thorns where they are stifled and cannot grow, and some on good soil where they are nurtured into what they are meant to be.

Our messages to our adolescents can also fall on any of these places in their hearts. As we continue to work on our relationships with our teenagers and keep planting seeds, there is more possibility that these seeds will fall into good soil and produce wonderful fruit.

REFLECTIONS

A. Do you think your teens care about your opinions?

Yes ☐   Somewhat ☐   No ☐

B. What makes you say that? _____

_____

C. What does it mean to you when your teens ask you for your thoughts/ feelings and take them into consideration?

_____

_____

D. How do you express this? _____

_____

E. What does it mean to you when your teens do not consider your views as relevant to their decision making process or their lives?

_____

_____

F. How do you share this? _____

_____

G. When you were growing up, did you care about what your parents thought and felt?

Yes ☐   Somewhat ☐   No ☐

H. How do you think this affects your perception and interaction with your teens today?

_____

_____

FROM KNOWLEDGE TO ACTION

A. Recognize that the way that your teens behave towards you is not necessarily what they feel on the inside. Do not just react to what you see and hear on the outside. Instead, respond to what you know to be true <u>in general</u>, not just in the moment of tension and conflict.

B. It is important to "plant seeds" in your teen. Your teaching, guidance, and advice that are built on love and justice are seeds that are planted in his heart. At some point, the seeds will take root, blossom, and become a healthy tree.

C. How do you prepare the soil that is your teen's heart so that the seeds do not just fly away, wither, or suffocate?

   1. At the risk of taking the metaphor too far, the soil is in a garden that needs to be tended well with necessary nutrients and items, e.g., sunlight, rain, fertilization, protection from animals, etc. What does this mean for a family?

     (a) Family environment that provides moderate levels of structure (boundaries and consequences) and high concentration of nurturance (warmth and support): This combination has been found to contribute strongly to engendering emotionally and relationally healthy kids.

     (b) Family time: Quality and quantity of time spent together via regular mealtimes where members share about their day, game nights where members have fun together, consistent family meetings where members can discuss their concerns/ wishes, weekend activities where they volunteer together to edify their community, etc.

     (c) No family "wars": While there may be disagreements and passionate discussions about issues, it is extremely stressful to have situations where family members are attacking each others' character, being hostile and contemptuous, or sustaining high levels of anger for days/weeks/months. It is really doubtful that anyone, let alone your teens, can listen and follow your guidance, under these conditions.

2. Engender trust, respect, and responsibility in your teens.

   (a) Model these in all your relationships.

   (b) Create opportunities for your teens to build trust in themselves, learn how they can navigate in their world, treat themselves and others with respect, and develop responsible choices.

3. Even as you seek to teach your teens, be willing to learn and grow too.

   (a) Communicate your willingness to understand your teens' generation and culture. In fact, reading this book is one way of demonstrating this.

   (b) Continue to increase your knowledge and skills sets. This can be related to your work, hobbies, sports, etc.

4. Practice what you preach.

   (a) If you want your teens to spend less time playing computer games and more time reading, perhaps you might turn off the computer and read also.

   (b) Your teens have an antenna for hypocritical behaviors and attitudes. Align your messages with your own actions.

Chapter 9

What Teens Want

*Name three things
teens want from parents.*

*O*ur children tell us what they want from us in obvious and subtle ways. Due to our hectic pace, stressful life, and not-so-lovely relationship with our teens at times, we may not be on the same frequency. Thus, on many occasions, we fail to hear their needs and wants. Much as they miss what we say, we also fail to hear what they say.

For those of us who have teens who know what they want and are persistent about asking for them, we may feel inundated by all of their wishes and lose track of the important needs. As a result, we end up not attending to these. On the opposite end of the spectrum, some of us have kids who are not really aware of what they want and take forever to decide on anything. In this case, we get frustrated and give up on encouraging them to share what they want from us. This, of course, then leads to not listening very well. All of these roads lead to a parent-teen disconnect.

As a mom, I have some ideas of what my teenagers want. You probably do too. However, I often wonder how my kids would prioritize their needs and wants. Do these align with what I want for them? Or what I think they need? And if they told me what they wanted, should I provide it?

WE WANT LOVE

In the survey, the top three things teens said they want from their parents are: love, money, and freedom. Who doesn't want to be loved? Everyone wants to feel loved. Teens may not always admit that they need their parents' love. But deep down, they long for this type of connection.

Knowing that there's always someone that has our back and genuinely cares for us means a lot – even if we don't acknowledge this to our parents. In fact, we may communicate the opposite at times. And parents react to this by "going away." Parents, please remember that we need the feeling of being loved and being close to you. While we might push you away with our words and actions when we feel like you are in our faces, we still need you to stand behind us.

WE WANT MONEY

In addition to love, of course, teens want money. In order to hang out these days, money is required. It's hard to be a teenager without money: In fact, you may soon find yourself being left out of things if you don't have money. Parents may feel used, because we ask for money all the time, but for some teens, it's a way to try to connect with their parents. Maybe asking and receiving money is the only way they know how to strike up a conversation or to feel loved.

Teens aren't the only ones who use money to build a friendship or relationship. I know parents who use money to "win" their child's affection. Instead of spending time talking or doing stuff together, some parents just give money to their kids so that they can go back to doing what they want and not be bothered.

WE WANT FREEDOM

Every teen also needs freedom. Although we understand and acknowledge that having rules is necessary for life, we still don't like having restrictions. It feels great to do what we want. Even if we act without thinking and do something we shouldn't, we can use these as opportunities to learn and grow.

We need to learn from our own mistakes sometimes instead of having our parents shelter us all the time. When parents are too strict and controlling, teens tend to lie and rebel. They may really get in trouble in these situations.

WE WANT MORE

Other wishes that teens in our survey stated are support, trust, stuff, approval, and privacy. I think these are all necessary for life and successful relationships in the future. My parents' support helps me to feel secure and loved. This makes it easier for me to express love to others. Along with support, trust is really important. Without trust, there's no relationship.

Teens also want things like iPods, cell phones, laptops, nice clothes (more the better), and cars. They want to be like everyone else who has these. In our world, "everyone" seems to have them. Parents may not always approve of the things that teens want. In addition, parents may not be able to afford them. These issues cause tension in the family.

Finally, I think by now you know that privacy is a big issue. My mom and I talked about this in the previous chapters. Overall, I guess what teens want is more relational rather than material things. That's good, right?

"RELATIONAL" IS GREAT

Yes! It is really wonderful news that teens are more concerned with the relational aspects of their lives with their parents rather than with acquisition of possessions through their parents. One can cause parents to experience a person-to-person relationship with their teens while the other can lead parents to feel like objects to be used as needed. Depending on the degree to which teens might interact with their parents, their relationships may thrive or suffer.

"I-YOU" VS. "I-IT" RELATIONSHIPS

It is understandable that teens want money and things, such as clothing and electronic gadgets, because these communicate a certain image and status. However, if they place too high of an importance on obtaining material goods, they can develop difficulties with their parents. In this situation, adolescents may use parents as a means to an end.

This type of relationship is what the philosopher Martin Buber calls an "I-It" relationship.[29] Rather than an "I-You" relationship that emphasizes mutuality, authenticity, and dialogue, "I-It" relationship is characterized by objectification (the other is treated as an object to be used in service of one's own interests) and narcissism (the other is only a representation of oneself). This way of relating creates monologue, self-absorption, and disconnect.

As adolescents are maturing, it is normal for them to interact with their parents in this manner at times. As they develop into adulthood, it is essential that they relate to others more in an "I-You" position in order to be physically, psychologically, and spiritually healthy.

Adolescents who emphasize the importance of acquiring possessions not only have issues with others but also within themselves. In *Affluenza: The All-Consuming Epidemic,* De Graff, Wann & Naylor (2005) state, "We keep looking outside ourselves for satisfactions that can only come from within…happiness comes from achieving intrinsic goals like giving and receiving love…people with extrinsic goals sharpen their egos to conquer outer space, but they don't have a clue how to navigate inner space."[30]

Teenagers are more prone to searching outside of themselves as they are in the process of deciding who and what they will assimilate into their sense of self. Thus, it is imperative to encourage them to choose what they will incorporate from the external variables wisely and to focus on developing their internal character. If they concentrate too much on the external factors to fuel their self-worth, they are in danger of becoming more self-absorbed, feeling depressed, engaging in maladaptive coping strategies, and having less meaningful connections.[31]

On the other hand, if adolescents desire relational intangibles that nurture their sense of self, they are more likely to develop healthier identities and ways of connecting with their world. Many of the teens in our survey state that they want love from their parents. What they are seeking is unconditional love: The feeling of being loved for who they are, not what they do. This kind of love results in a sense of emotional attachment and security that allows for a healthy exploration of the self.

Kids are also asking for freedom to make their own choices and to forge their own paths. It is necessary to expand the boundaries within which parents allow their children to discover and interact with their world as they get older. This encourages them to develop their own identities and values that are informed by – and not mindlessly adopted from – their parents and other significant individuals in their lives. This is essential in building a solid, stable foundation from which they can make healthy decisions in various arenas of their lives. Development of authentic relationships is based on such experiences of freedom, trust, support, and love.

LISTENING MINDFULLY

Underlying these wishes is the fundamental need to be heard. Do parents hear their kids? Sometimes. How can parents increase the likelihood that they are attending to what their children are expressing? Listen mindfully: Focus on nonjudgmental awareness of thoughts, feelings, and sensory experiences when hearing. This refers to listening without analyzing, reacting, or judging.

Being mindful in various circumstances (e.g., eating, walking, listening) has been correlated with various positive benefits: physically, mentally, emotionally, and relationally. For example, researchers at Massachusetts General Hospital and Harvard Medical School have found that the brains of those who consistently engage in a specific protocol of mindful meditation reveal positive structural differences in the areas of the brain associated with learning, memory, self-awareness, and empathy.[32] Clearly, increases in these parameters can facilitate parent-teen relationships.

When we listen to our teenagers, how often do we interrupt to begin talking about our perspectives? How often do we think about how we will respond while they are speaking? How often do we walk away frustrated by the interchanges? Most of us are guilty of behaving in ways that decrease effective communication with our kids.

Listening mindfully means that we are in the here-and-now, aware of our own internal processes even as we are conscious of theirs, without evaluating, reacting, or criticizing what we are hearing. When parents listen mindfully, they become more physically and emotionally attuned to what is being conveyed by their adolescents. This can lead to healthier connections.

REFLECTIONS

A. What do your teens want from you?

_____

B. How do you know what they desire?   _____

_____

_____

C. Are you providing what they wish?

Yes ☐   Sometimes ☐   No ☐

Why or why not?   _____

_____

_____

D. How much of your connection with your teenagers is based on provision of material goods?

Think about your interactions even just today or this week as you answer this question.

Little ☐   Some ☐   A Lot ☐

E. How does this affect the quality of your relationship?   _____

_____

_____

F. Do you observe a correlation between your teens' hunger for material possessions and their self-image?

Yes ☐ No ☐

If yes, in what ways? _____

_____

_____

G. How much of your connection with your teens is based on mutual love, trust, support, etc.?

Think about your interactions even just today or this week as you answer this question.

Little ☐ Some ☐ A Lot ☐

H. How does this affect the quality of your relationship? _____

_____

_____

I. Do you notice a link between your teens' desire for nurturance and their self-image?

Yes ☐ No ☐

If yes, in what ways? _____

_____

_____

FROM KNOWLEDGE TO ACTION

A. It is crucial to know what your teens want from you and to provide what is necessary for their physical and psychological well-being.

B. Before you can really hear your teens, you need to first practice listening to yourself. In order to have healthy relationships, it is critical to distinguish what messages are coming from within yourself vs. others. It is necessary to hone your listening skills by training yourself to pay attention to what is occurring by yourself first prior to learning how to do this while interacting with others.

C. Practice the following:

1. Make yourself physically comfortable.

2. Engage in Deep Breathing (taught in a previous chapter).

3. Quiet your mind to only hear what is in the present. Pay attention to what is happening in and around you: What sounds do you hear? What sensations do you have? What do you feel?

4. Let these flow in and out through your awareness without analysis or judgment. If you are new to mindful listening, you can start with one minute of practice and then gradually lengthen this time to about 20 minutes.

D. When listening to your teenagers:

1. Be in a physical position that is comfortable for you and your teens.

2. Engage in Deep Breathing in order to be in a relaxed state which helps to focus your thoughts on your teens and not react emotionally to their messages.

3. Listen only to what they are telling you. Do not interrupt, evaluate, or criticize.

E. Once you have listened, you can reflect back to them what you heard to clarify and understand exactly what is being conveyed. This communicates your awareness of who your kids are and what they are needing, which then, encourages your teenagers to be more open to hearing what you have to share afterward.

Finale

Parent-Teen Connections

The following is a story[33] from the Native American Sno-homish people in the Pacific Northwest:

When the Creator made the world, he made many different groups of people and gave them all different languages to speak. They couldn't talk to one another, but they did agree about one thing. They didn't like one thing the Creator had done: He'd put the sky so low that the tall people were bumping their heads up against it.

One day all the wise men and women from all the different tribes got together and decided they should lift up the sky. They talked and talked about how to do it, until finally they understood one another well enough to make a plan. All the creatures of the earth should get together, they said, and try to push up the sky. If all the people and animals and birds could push at the same time, they said, the sky would move up.

"But we all speak different languages," one of the wise men reminded the others. "How will we know when to push?" The wise ones talked and talked until at last they agreed on how to signal to one another. When it was the right time to push, they decided that someone should shout, "Ya-ho." That was the word that meant "everybody lift together" in all the different Indian languages. The wise ones told the plan to all the people and all the animals and all the birds. The people cut down giant fir trees to use as poles that could push up the sky.

Soon the big day came. The people all raised their poles so that the tips were just barely

*touching the sky. Then the wise ones shouted,
"Ya-ho!" Everybody pushed, and the sky moved
up a little bit. They shouted again, everybody
pushed again, and the sky moved up a little bit
more. The wise ones kept on shouting "Ya-ho!"
and everybody kept pushing together, pushing
and pushing until the sky moved up just as high
as it is now.*

Sometimes it can feel as if there just is not enough space
in the house to accommodate both you and your teens. You
bump against and collide with your teenagers' thoughts and
feelings, and vice versa.

Like the people in the story who felt pressed in by their
environment, you and your teenagers may feel squashed and
conflicted by the other's seemingly stronger voice, approach,
and personality. If you work to clear the community space
of your own agendas and emotional hurts, you increase the
possibility that you can co-exist relatively peacefully and
joyfully.

Other times, it can feel as if you and your kids are
speaking different languages. The characters in the story
could not understand each other. However, they kept trying
to communicate, and eventually, they were able to unite
together as a community to make life easier for everyone.

Even if your relationship with your teens feels too
difficult, exhausting, and painful, it is ultimately rewarding
to stay engaged with them. It is important to continue to
dialogue with your teenagers. Reading this book is one of the
steps you have taken to encourage and "push" for connection
with your kids.

This work has been, in one way or another, about
attending to who our kids are and what they care about.
What have you learned? What have you been reminded of?

In many ways, our adolescents are much like us: We all long to be known, accepted, and loved. We yearn to connect.

How these desires are manifested may be different between us and our kids – given the cognitive, affective, and behavioral dimensions of the various developmental stages. Understanding both the difference in the process (how we are where we are) as well as the sameness in purpose (where we want to be) provides the first significant step towards building a lasting, intimate relationship with one another.

You have been given an opportunity to glimpse the adolescent world with our *Guest Pass*. We have visited our teens' world in order to appreciate their interests, struggles, and hopes. We trust that you have found your "tour" to be meaningful and valuable.

While it may be difficult to apply all that you have read into practice, if you start with one note, you can begin to create a melody. We encourage you to take one lesson, one tool, one piece of knowledge and make it real in your lives with your teens. Eventually, that one change will lead to other transformations, creating healthier connections between you and your teenagers.

Acknowledgements

Many people have contributed to the process and completion of this book. We are tremendously grateful for the love, support, and encouragement of all of our family and friends.

Thank you, Chris Cha, for your trust and confidence in us to write this book. Brannon Cha, we appreciate your compassion, knowledge, and wit. Your clever observations about the teen's world were not only useful but entertaining as well.

Sun and Paul Oh, your continuous prayers and belief in us laid the foundation for writing this mother-daughter book. Thank you for empowering us to make our dream a reality. Carolyn Taketa, your insightful questions and incisive comments facilitated further refining of this book. Thank you for all the time and effort spent on reading, listening, and sharing. Maria Lloyd, thank you for reading the drafts and giving valuable feedback. We appreciate your generosity in imparting your knowledge of the writing and publishing process. Dariel Doyle, your total enthusiasm for our writing motivated us to continue pushing through until the end. You are a fabulous cheerleader and editor.

Thank you to all the teens who completed our survey. Your open and honest responses provided information that enriched our book. A special thanks to those of you who gave us permission to use your comments/stories.

Much love and gratitude to our close friends who

enhance our lives: *from Susan* – Cindy, Sami, Hyo, Linda, and Inseong, and *from Yumi* – you know who you are. To our wonderful "home group," thank you for your prayers.

Most of all, we thank God for being with us throughout this journey. Without God's inspiration, wisdom, and guidance, this book would never have been realized.

References

1. Children's Health Council. (2010). *Internet & teens: parenting in the age of texting, sexting, gaming, & facebook.* Palo Alto, California.
2. O'Koon, J. (1997). Attachment to parents and peers in late adolescence and their relationship with self-image. *Adolescence, 32,* 471-482.
3 Joinson, A. (2001). Revelations on the internet. *The British Psychological Society, London Conference, Institute of Education Press Release.* Retrieved from http://www.bps.org.uk/media-centre/press-releases/releases$/london-conferencelectures/revelations-on-the-internet$.cfm
4. Thompson, P. (2004). Imaging study shows brain maturing. *UCLA Laboratory of Neuroimaging Press Release.* Retrieved from http://www.nimh.nih.gov/science-news/2004/imaging-study-shows-brain-maturing.shtml
5. Merikangas, K. R., He, J., Burstein, M., Swanson, S. A., Avenevoli, S., Cui, L., Benjet, C., Georgiades, K., & Swendsen, J. (2010). Lifetime prevalence of mental disorders in U.S. adolescents: Results from the national comorbidity survey replication - adolescent supplement (NCS-A). *Journal of the American Academy of Child & Adolescent Psychiatry, 49*(10),

980-989.

6. American Psychiatric Association. (1994). *Diagnostic and statistical manual of mental disorders* (4th ed.).Washington DC: Author.

7. Pennebaker, J. W. (1997). *Opening up: The healing power of expressing emotions.* New York: Guildford Press.

8. Levinson, R., & Ruef, A. (1992). Empathy: A physiological substrate. *Journal of Personality and Social Psychology, 63,* 234-246.

9. Barsade, S. G. (2002). The ripple effect: Emotional contagion and its influence on group behavior. *Administrative Science Quarterly, 47*(4), 644-675.

10. Whitlock, J. L., Powers, J. L., & Eckenrode, J. (2006). The virtual cutting edge: The internet and adolescent self-injury. *Developmental Psychology, 42*(3), 407-417.

11. Masten, A. S. (2009). Ordinary magic: lessons from research on resilience in human development. *Education Canada, 49*(3), 28-32.

12. American Psychological Association (2002). *Developing adolescents: Reference for professionals.* Washington DC: Author.

13. Jaccard, J., Blanton, H., & Dodge, T. (2005). Peer influences on risk behavior: An analysis of the effects of a close friend. *Developmental Psychology, 41*(1), 135-147.

14. American Psychological Association. (2011). *Resilience for teens: Got bounce?* Retrieved from http://www.apa.org/helpcenter/bounce.aspx#

15. Philippians 4:6 (New Living Translation Bible) Don't worry about anything; instead, pray about everything. Tell God what you need, and thank him for all he has done.

16. Leviticus 19:28 (New International Version Bible) Do not cut your bodies for the dead or put tattoo marks

on yourselves. I am the LORD.

17. Public Health Agency of Canada: Youth Culture Inc. (2001). *Special report on youth, piercing, tattooing and Hepatitis C trendscan findings*. Retrieved from http://www.phac-aspc.gc.ca/hepc/pubs/youthpt-jeunessept/index-eng.php

18. Carroll, S. T., Riffenburgh, R. H., Roberts, T. A., & Myhre, E. B. (2002). Tattoos and body piercings as indicators of adolescent risk-taking behaviors. *Pediatrics, 109*(6), 1021-1027.

19. American Psychological Assocation. (2007). *Report of the APA task force on the sexualization of girls*. Retrieved from http://www.apa.org/pi/women/programs/girls/report.aspx

20. Fredrickson, B. L., Robers, T. A., Noll, S. M., Quinn, D. M., & Twenge, J. M. (1998). That swimsuit becomes you: sex differences in self-objectification, restrained eating, and math performance. *Journal of Personality and Social Psychology, 75*(1), 269-284.

21. Hebi, M. R., King, E. B., & Lin, J. (2004). The swimsuit becomes us all: ethnicity, gender, and vulnerability to self-objectification. *Personality and Social Psychology Bulletin, 30*(10), 1322-1331.

22. Teen Help.com. (2009). *Teen help: Teens that lie, steal and/or cheat*. Retrieved from http://blog.teenhelp.com/2009/11/teens-that-lie-steal-andor-cheat.html

23. Johnston, L. D., O'Malley, P. M., Bachman, J. G., & Schulenberg, J. E. (2010). *Monitoring the future. National survey results on drug use, 1975–2009: Volume I, secondary school students* (NIHPublication No. 10-7584). Bethesda, MD: National Institute on Drug Abuse.

24. Substance Abuse and Mental Health Services Administration. (2010). *Results from the 2009 national survey on drug use and health: Volume I,*

Summary of national findings (Office of Applied Studies, NSDUH Series H-38A, HHS Publication No. SMA 10-4586 Findings). Rockville, MD.

25. National Center for Chronic Disease Prevention and Health Promotion, Division of Adolescent and School Health. (2010). *Healthy youth! Sexual risk behaviors.* Retrieved from http://www.cdc.gov/HealthyYouth/sexualbehaviors/index.htm

26. Kaiser Family Foundation. (2003). *National survey of adolescents and young adults: Sexual health knowledge, attitudes, and behaviors.* Menlo Park: Author.

27. Albert, B. (2004). *With one voice: America's adults and teens sound off about teen pregnancy.* Washington, DC: National Campaign to Prevent Teen Pregnancy.

28. Bibby, R. W. & Penner, J. (2010). *Ten things we all need to know about today's teens.* Lethbridge, Canada: Project Canada Books.

29. Buber, M. (1970). *I and Thou.* New York: Charles Scribner's Sons. (Translated by Walter Kaufmann).

30. De Graff, J., Wann, D., & Naylor, T. H. (2005). *Affluenza: The all-consuming epidemic.* San Francisco: Berrett-Koehler Publishers, Inc.

31. Schor, J. B. (2004). *Born to buy: The commercialized child and the new consumer culture.* New York: Scribner.

32. Holzel, B. K., Carmody, J., Vangel, M., Congleton, C., Yerramsetti, S. M., Gard, T., & Lazar, S. (2011). Mindfulness practice leads to increases in regional brain gray matter density. *Psychiatry Research: Neuroimaging, 191*(1), 36-43.

33. Fitzpatrick, J. G. (1998). *Once upon a family: Read-aloud stories and activities that nurture healthy kids.* New York: Viking.

About the Authors

Susan Oh Cha, Ph.D. is a licensed clinical psychologist. She has worked in various treatment settings: university counseling centers, hospitals, community mental health agencies, and private practice. She is committed to facilitating healing and wholeness in individuals and relationships. She has given numerous lectures and workshops on parenting and developmental issues, especially related to teens. She also consults with organizations and engages in community outreach. Dr. Cha is currently in private practice with a group of multi-disciplinary mental health practitioners. Her clinical work consists of helping individuals, couples, and families struggling with mood disorders, anxiety disorders, family discord, cross-cultural issues, and spiritual concerns.

Yumi Bryana Cha is a junior in high school. She is interested in studying psychology. This is due in part to her natural role in her friendships: Many peers have approached her with their problems, and Yumi finds it rewarding to encourage her friends as they work through their struggles, especially with their parents. She has been a part of various organizations, such as People to People Student Ambassador Program, California Youth Symphony, Girl Scouts, JRP Acting and Modeling School, and Key Club. Yumi also has a Black Belt in Tae Kwon Do, sings in her school's chamber choir and in her church's praise team, and plays multiple musical instruments. The best part about all these life experiences, in her opinion, is meeting people who then become wonderful friends.

.

CPSIA information can be obtained at www.ICGtesting.com
Printed in the USA
269958BV00005B/3/P